PYGMALION

Other titles in the Greenhaven Press Literary Companion Series:

British Authors

Jane Austen
Joseph Conrad
Charles Dickens
J.R.R. Tolkien

British Literature

Animal Farm
Beowulf
Brave New World
The Canterbury Tales
A Christmas Carol
Great Expectations
Gulliver's Travels
Hamlet
Heart of Darkness
The Importance of Being Earnest
Jane Eyre
Julius Caesar
Lord of the Flies
Macbeth
The Merchant of Venice
A Midsummer Night's Dream
Oliver Twist
Othello
A Portrait of the Artist as a Young Man
Pride and Prejudice
Romeo and Juliet
Shakespeare: The Comedies
Shakespeare: The Histories
Shakespeare: The Sonnets
Shakespeare: The Tragedies
Silas Marner
A Tale of Two Cities
The Taming of the Shrew
Tess of the d'Urbervilles
Twelfth Night
Wuthering Heights

THE GREENHAVEN PRESS
Literary Companion
TO BRITISH LITERATURE

READINGS ON

PYGMALION

Gary Wiener, *Book Editor*

Daniel Leone, *President*
Bonnie Szumski, *Publisher*
Scott Barbour, *Managing Editor*

Greenhaven Press, Inc., San Diego, CA

Library of Congress Cataloging-in-Publication Data

Readings on Pygmalion / Gary Wiener, book editor.
        p. cm. — (The Greenhaven Press literary
companion to British literature)
        Includes bibliographical references and index.
        ISBN 0-7377-0191-9 (alk. paper) —
ISBN 0-7377-0190-0 (pbk. : alk. paper)
        1. Shaw, George Bernard, 1856–1950. Pygmalion.
I. Wiener, Gary. II. Series.

PR5363.P83 R43   2002
822'.912—dc21   2001042925
                                                    CIP

Cover photo: © Hulton/Archive by Getty Images

Copyright © 2002 by Greenhaven Press,
an imprint of The Gale Group
10911 Technology Place
San Diego, CA 92127
Printed in the U.S.A.

"The English have no respect for their language, and will not teach their children to speak it. They spell it so abominably that no man can teach himself what it sounds like."

—George Bernard Shaw

Contents

Chapter 1: Background on *Pygmalion*

Shaw specifically wrote the part of Eliza for the famed—and notorious—actress, Mrs. Stella Patrick Campbell after seeing her perform on stage one night. But how to get a renowned diva to play the role of a poor guttersnipe was another matter altogether. Despite Shaw's trepidation, after hearing him read the script, Mrs. Campbell was happy to accept the role of Eliza Doolittle.

With a war looming, battles between the playwright and the actors, a lead actor who played Henry Higgins miserably, and a grandmother of forty-nine trying to play an eighteen-year-old girl, the opening night of *Pygmalion* was chiefly remarkable for the sensation caused by a single word. When Eliza says *bloody* on stage, everyone from critics to real flower girls has an opinion regarding the appropriateness of the foul utterance.

Chapter 2: Characters

Henry Higgins has all of the superficial trappings of a gentleman, but his conduct is unbecoming of one. The true gentleman of the play is the soft-spoken Colonel Pickering, from whose conduct Eliza learns proper etiquette. Yet the true artisan of Eliza's transformation is Higgins. The final acts of the play depict a battle between the coldly professional mentor and the warm-hearted pupil, but neither is wholly victorious.

Henry Higgins, whose excessive admiration for a perfect mother renders him incapable of loving another woman, must invariably be both a harsh and attractive figure. He is incorrigible—incapable of changing into a softer man—and the entire plot of *Pygmalion* confirms his anti-romanticism. Each act of the play initially develops a romantic situation, then dashes the hope of an improbable romantic conclusion.

Chapter 3: Themes and Technique

edy of his speeches, but it also suggests a man who, despite his low social standing, is capable of operating on a higher plane.

Chapter 4: Reviews and Continuing Reception

FOREWORD

*"'Tis the good reader that
makes the good book."*

Ralph Waldo Emerson

The story's bare facts are simple: The captain, an old and scarred seafarer, walks with a peg leg made of whale ivory. He relentlessly drives his crew to hunt the world's oceans for the great white whale that crippled him. After a long search, the ship encounters the whale and a fierce battle ensues. Finally the captain drives his harpoon into the whale, but the harpoon line catches the captain about the neck and drags him to his death.

A simple story, a straightforward plot—yet, since the 1851 publication of Herman Melville's *Moby-Dick*, readers and critics have found many meanings in the struggle between Captain Ahab and the whale. To some, the novel is a cautionary tale that depicts how Ahab's obsession with revenge leads to his insanity and death. Others believe that the whale represents the unknowable secrets of the universe and that Ahab is a tragic hero who dares to challenge fate by attempting to discover this knowledge. Perhaps Melville intended Ahab as a criticism of Americans' tendency to become involved in well-intentioned but irrational causes. Or did Melville model Ahab after himself, letting his fictional character express his anger at what he perceived as a cruel and distant god?

Although literary critics disagree over the meaning of *Moby-Dick*, readers do not need to choose one particular interpretation in order to gain an understanding of Melville's novel. Instead, by examining various analyses, they can gain numerous insights into the issues that lie under the surface of the basic plot. Studying the writings of literary critics can also aid readers in making their own assessments of *Moby-Dick* and other literary works and in developing analytical thinking skills.

The Greenhaven Literary Companion Series was created with these goals in mind. Designed for young adults, this unique anthology series provides an engaging and comprehensive introduction to literary analysis and criticism. The essays included in the Literary Companion Series are chosen for their accessibility to a young adult audience and are expertly edited in consideration of both the reading and comprehension levels of this audience. In addition, each essay is introduced by a concise summation that presents the contributing writer's main themes and insights. Every anthology in the Literary Companion Series contains a varied selection of critical essays that cover a wide time span and express diverse views. Wherever possible, primary sources are represented through excerpts from authors' notebooks, letters, and journals and through contemporary criticism.

Each title in the Literary Companion Series pays careful consideration to the historical context of the particular author or literary work. In-depth biographies and detailed chronologies reveal important aspects of authors' lives and emphasize the historical events and social milieu that influenced their writings. To facilitate further research, every anthology includes primary and secondary source bibliographies of articles and/or books selected for their suitability for young adults. These engaging features make the Greenhaven Literary Companion Series ideal for introducing students to literary analysis in the classroom or as a library resource for young adults researching the world's great authors and literature.

Exceptional in its focus on young adults, the Greenhaven Literary Companion Series strives to present literary criticism in a compelling and accessible format. Every title in the series is intended to spark readers' interest in leading American and world authors, to help them broaden their understanding of literature, and to encourage them to formulate their own analyses of the literary works that they read. It is the editors' hope that young adult readers will find these anthologies to be true companions in their study of literature.

INTRODUCTION

George Bernard Shaw's *Pygmalion* is one of those works of art that, like Eliza Doolittle herself, has overcome its lowly beginnings. Shaw himself did not originally place much importance on it, labeling the play a "potboiler," a piece written solely to make money. Shaw's original intent with *Pygmalion*, which tells the tale of a linguistics professor who attempts to turn a lower-class girl into a flawless society woman, was educational. Shaw believed that the English people could not speak their own language and wanted to introduce the science of phonetics to the general public as a means toward ameliorating the problem. Though audiences fell in love with the play's romantic plot and the interaction between Henry and Liza, Shaw was attempting to convey a didactic message to the audience in support of Henry Higgins's wish for a more exact alphabet that would capture the actual sounds of the English language. In his will, Shaw devoted a sum of money to ensure that studies would go forth in order to assess the viability of adopting a new forty-letter alphabet. He even went so far as to have one play, *Androcles and the Lion*, transcribed into this alphabet, and copies can be found in libraries to this day, with Shaw's alphabet on the lefthand side of the page and English on the right.

But *Pygmalion*, with its unmistakable likeness to the Cinderella tale, gained a life of its own on the stage and, ultimately, as the wildly successful musical *My Fair Lady*. Though critics have never considered *Pygmalion* one of Shaw's great works, and have preferred his much more complex and deeply philosophical plays such as *Back to Methuselah* and *Man and Superman*, *Pygmalion* has become, arguably, the most famous and popular work of his long writing career.

The play has defied Shaw's intentions in one other way as well. For years, Shaw steadfastly refused to allow Eliza and Henry to enact that most romantic of endings, the seemingly inevitable happily-ever-after conclusion that his audience craved. Herbert Tree, who directed the first London production and starred as Henry Higgins, pleaded with Shaw to devise an ending in which the former flower girl and her irascible mentor fall in love. Shaw refused, so Tree made subtle changes in the action to suggest a future romance between Henry and Eliza. When Shaw objected, Tree said, "My ending makes money: you ought to be grateful." Shaw responded, "Your ending is damnable. You ought to be shot." In an attempt to combat such theatrical heresy, Shaw wrote a prose "sequel" to *Pygmalion* that married the strong-willed Eliza off to her love-stricken suitor, Freddy Eynsford Hill. But actors, directors, producers, and theatergoers alike ultimately had their way with the production of the film version of *Pygmalion* (1938) and the musical *My Fair Lady*, the endings of which imply that Eliza will come back to live with Higgins in some ambiguous fashion.

It is not hard to see why *Pygmalion* has become so popular with audiences. Eliza Doolittle and Henry Higgins are among the most delightful and engaging characters in twentieth-century theater. *Pygmalion's* plot, a simple tale of overcoming one's social class, is enlivened not only by the engaging interplay of Eliza and Higgins, but by the rich cast of supporting characters that includes Eliza's hilarious father, Alfred Doolittle; Henry's perfect mother, Mrs. Higgins; and that scrupulous gentleman Colonel Pickering. The dialogue is witty throughout, and certain scenes, such as the one at Mrs. Higgins's home during which Eliza first tries to speak as an English lady and fails miserably, are absolutely brilliant comedy.

The story of Pygmalion derives from Roman mythology, as told by Ovid in his tale of change, *The Metamorphoses*. According to the myth, Pygmalion, a sculptor from the island of Cypress, was a woman hater. Resolving never to marry, he instead spent all of his time working on a statue of a woman, and he ultimately fell in love with his creation. This unrequited love, for no statue can return a man's love, sent Pygmalion into deep depression. The goddess Venus, hearing of his plight and fascinated by a new type of love, turns the statue into a living, breathing woman. Venus herself attends the marriage ceremony of Pygmalion and the statue-turned-woman, whom he had named Galatea.

Shaw was not the first author of his era to appropriate the

Pygmalion myth and fashion it into a story about modern English life. Several prominent adaptations were current before Shaw created his version. This is not unusual in the playwrighting world, however. Several versions of *Hamlet* were produced in the era just before Shakespeare wrote his own. In such cases, it is the playwright's unique vision of romance and reality, and a rare genius in the creation of plot, character, and dialogue, that raises one author's version above all others.

George Bernard Shaw: A Biography

George Bernard Shaw once asserted that there was little reason to write his biography:

> I have had no heroic adventures. Things have not happened to me: on the contrary it is I who have happened to them; and all my happenings have taken the form of books and plays. Read them or spectate them; and you have my whole story; the rest is only breakfast, lunch, dinner, sleeping, wakening, and washing, my routine being just the same as everybody's routine.

These are very self-effacing words from a man who was not only a great British writer but also a music, art, and theater critic, public official, orator, activist, and international celebrity. If that is not achievement enough, Shaw is generally regarded as the finest English playwright since William Shakespeare.

Shaw was a unique and paradoxical figure, whose witty and satirical nature must have stemmed in part from being brought up by an inept and ineffective father and an indifferent and unresponsive mother. In later years Shaw would go so far as to reject his given name of "George," which he shared with his father, often instructing those who referred to him by this name, "Don't George me." He instead constructed the persona of G.B.S., a charismatic and flamboyant intellectual who faced an ever-changing and complex world with a razor-sharp wit and a worldview that mixed high seriousness with uproarious comedy.

His ironic and sizzling sense of humor was well known. His witticisms rank with those of Mark Twain and Oscar Wilde. For example, it was Shaw who first wrote, "He who can, does. He who cannot, teaches." After the successful premiere of *Arms and the Man*, standing amid the effusive applause of the audience, he turned to a lone heckler and said, "I quite agree with you sir. But what can two do against so many?" And as the story goes, when the rotund film director Alfred Hitchcock said, "One look at you, Mr. Shaw, and I know there's a famine in the land," the lean playwright replied, "One look at you, Mr. Hitchcock, and I know who caused it."

Shaw lived ninety-four years, his life spanning the heyday of ultrarespectable, conformist Victorianism through the postatomic era following World War II. His plays continually challenged societal norms and forced audiences to confront the most difficult issues of the day. But almost always he retained his optimistic vision, as he charted the human comedy like no other playwright of his time.

CHILDHOOD IN DUBLIN

George Bernard Shaw was born in Dublin, Ireland, on July 26, 1856, the third child of Lucinda and George Shaw. Lucinda Elizabeth Shaw, known as Bessie, had married George Carr Shaw, a man nearly twice her age, out of desperation. With her mother dead and her father a ne'er-do-well who lived off others, Bessie had been reared by her maternal aunt, Miss Ellen Whitcroft. By the time Bessie was seventeen, she found her aunt's austere religious upbringing intolerable. She had been hoping to return to her father's home, but when Miss Whitcroft learned, through Bessie, that her father was planning to remarry a woman whose debts he had paid off with money borrowed from Whitcroft herself, she had him arrested for debt on his wedding day. Forced to remain with her aunt, Bessie instead opted for marriage in June 1852, and was promptly cut out of Miss Whitcroft's will.

Bessie's choice of husband was, by all accounts, not a wise one. Shaw's father, George Carr Shaw, brought with him an impressive heritage but little else. His second cousin was Sir Robert Shaw, a baronet (a British hereditary title ranking below that of baron) who lived in Bushy Park, outside of Dublin. George Carr Shaw had used his family connections to gain employment in the Dublin law courts despite his knowing nothing about the law. But he had been laid off before meeting Bessie, and was granted a pension of sixty pounds a year. He promptly traded in this pension for five hundred pounds in cash, which he used to go into business running a flour mill, another occupation of which he had no knowledge.

Bessie Shaw had three children—Lucinda Frances (Lucy), Elinor Agnes (Yuppy), and George Bernard (Sonny)—within four years. But while she lavished love on the girls, she offered little emotional support to George and even less to her husband, her disdain for whom certainly stemmed in part from his alcoholism. One morning, while walking with his son, George Carr Shaw pretended to throw Sonny into a nearby canal. When Sonny returned home, he voiced to Bessie Shaw his suspicion that his father might be drunk, to which she retorted, "Ah, when is he anything else?" In later years Shaw would point to this realization early in his life as shattering his illusion of childhood innocence. As an adult, he wrote the famous actress Ellen Terry of this incident, claiming "I have never believed in anything since."

Nevertheless, George Carr Shaw carried a high opinion of himself. As a member of the Irish Protestant upper class (descended from English and Scots who had settled in Ireland in the 1600s) who had fallen on hard financial times, he still considered himself genteel, above menial occupations. Biographer Sally Peters writes that "Sonny was taught to despise the worker but to respect the gentleman, even when gentility had been lost to poverty." Shaw would go on to see the irony in such foolish beliefs. In *Pygmalion*, he would satirize genteel poverty in the form of Freddy Eynsford Hill, Eliza's proper-but-impoverished suitor who lacks even the money to take Eliza for a taxi ride when she runs off from the Higgins establishment at the conclusion of act 4.

THE INFLUENCE OF GEORGE VANDELEUR LEE

Bessie Shaw cared little for either her husband or her children, but she found solace in music. She had, by all accounts, a beautiful mezzosoprano voice, and she drew the attention of a self-styled music teacher and charlatan, George Vandeleur Lee. Lee, a dark-haired, bearded man who walked with a limp, had devised a voice-training system that was reputed to keep a singer's voice pure until old age. In 1866, Lee moved in with the Shaws and, in the absence of a strong male presence, became the dominant early male figure in Shaw's life. As biographer Michael Holroyd writes, Shaw

> was dazzled by Lee and adopted many of his startling ideas—
> everything from sleeping with the windows open, to eating
> brown bread instead of white and parading his disdain for

all professional men: doctors, lawyers, academics and the like. Lee filled the house with music and banished family prayers.

There has always been speculation, however slim, that Lee, whom Shaw would later describe as "a mesmeric conductor and daringly original teacher of singing," was Shaw's father. Shaw conducted something of a lifelong campaign to insist that he was not the son of Vandeleur Lee. Biographer Michael Holroyd suggests that the plot of *Pygmalion* figures prominently in this campaign. The relationship of mentor Henry Higgins and pupil Eliza Doolittle bears some affinity to that of Vandeleur Lee and Bessie Shaw. Shaw's steadfast refusal to allow any romantic liaison between the teacher and pupil in the play is said by Holroyd to be "Shaw's restatement of Bessie's unromantic attachment to Lee."

There were benefits to growing up in a house in which music was a constant presence. As biographer Hesketh Pearson writes:

> The musical activities of his family were the most important part of Shaw's education. . . . Operas, concerts and oratorios were constantly being rehearsed at home and before he was fifteen he knew by heart many works by the great masters, from Handel and Beethoven to Verdi and [French composer Charles] Gounod.

George could whistle such compositions in their entirety. Bessie Shaw refused to teach Shaw the piano, so he learned how to play by himself. His father, too, refused to provide him with formal music lessons, afraid that his son would disgrace the family by becoming a professional musician. The result was that Shaw was almost entirely self-taught in music.

Shaw's formal education was sporadic and uneven. For a time he attended a poorly run, inexpensive school that catered to the gentry, which treated its pupils so poorly that he would in later years label it a "futile boy prison." But Vandeleur Lee insisted on a different school, one that catered to the sons of Catholic tradesmen. Shaw, however, was so embarrassed by having to attend school with supposed inferiors that he soon prevailed upon his parents to transfer him to yet another school. Disdaining formal education, Shaw rejected the books his schoolmasters forced on him. Instead, he became an insatiable reader of books that piqued his interest. He loved stirring tales such as *The Arabian Nights* and "The Ancient Mariner." He also enjoyed Shakespeare and

Dickens, both of whose works he read voraciously. "I pity the man who cannot enjoy Shakespeare," he wrote.

By the age of sixteen Shaw left school for the world of work. His father's connections enabled him to secure a clerk's position in the office of Uniacke Townsend, a leading Dubliner, where he soon impressed his superiors with his competence. But a few years later, when another, less competent employee was promoted over Shaw, he quit his job. George Vandeleur Lee had left Dublin for the more promising lure of London, and Bessie had followed him, taking the two girls but leaving her son and husband to fend for themselves. Hoping to make his way in the world, Shaw packed his bags at the age of nineteen and left for England.

LONDON

The nineteen-year-old Shaw found London initially no more hospitable than Dublin. Bessie had been working for Vandeleur Lee, teaching his singing method. But she soon realized that his tactics of luring wealthy women to devote their daughters to his training had at least as much to do with con artistry as it did with music. Bessie set out to teach vocal lessons of her own, but her meager earnings were not enough to improve the family fortunes. When Shaw came to live with Bessie and the two girls, he was not warmly welcomed, but seen as another burden. Shaw turned to Vandeleur Lee, under whose guidance he served as a ghost-writer of musical criticism that the master himself disliked writing. But Shaw's reviews were often so harsh that soon no one would accept them. He tried his hand at freelance writing, but sold little and earned no substantial income. In 1879 he succumbed to family pressure and took a job at the Edison Telephone Company. Only six months later, convinced he was unsuited to the workaday world, Shaw quit, vowing he would never again "sin against his nature by attempting to make an honest living."

On quitting his job in 1879, Shaw decided to become a novelist. He continued to live with his mother and sister Lucy (his other sister, Elinor, died of tuberculosis in 1876). This arrangement caused much friction in the family because he brought in no income. Instead, he produced five written pages a day, every day of the year without fail. His steady labor resulted in five novels over the next several years. They were, in order of composition, *Immaturity*, *The*

Irrational Knot, Love Among the Artists, Cashel Byron's Profession, and *An Unsocial Socialist.* Shaw submitted these novels to publishers all over England and America, but none was accepted. Though *Immaturity* was, in most later critics' eyes, aptly named, the novels that followed all suggested a high level of literary talent, but were ultimately rejected because they flouted conventional Victorian values. In their rebellion against prevailing cultural tradition and their creation of strong individual, free-thinking characters, these novels show many of the traits that would be evident in Shaw's plays. And though none were published in book form until Shaw's name as a playwright made them saleable, the novels were a necessary apprenticeship for the budding literary genius. "If I had never written the five long novels and the bushels of articles that were refused," Shaw in later years wrote in a letter, "I should not have been able to do the work [i.e., the plays] that finally offered itself to me."

BECOMING A SOCIALIST

During his early years in London, Shaw embarked on a self-improvement plan that prompted numerous changes in his personal life. With little formal education to fall back on and no social promise, Shaw was very much like his creation Eliza Doolittle. And like Eliza, Shaw was driven; in London, he went about the business of transforming himself. He found the reading room of the British Museum, and spent countless hours poring over books. He taught himself shorthand and studied languages and boxing. After reading negative comments on meat eating by English Romantic poet Percy Bysshe Shelley, Shaw became a vegetarian.

In an attempt to cast off a congenital shyness, in 1881 Shaw began to attend meetings of a debating club called the Zetetical Society (meaning "the seekers"). Here he forced himself to overcome his fears and engaged in rousing public debates on current issues such as atheism and evolution. The first paper he presented for debate was on the merits of the death penalty over life imprisonment. Shaw soon developed a reputation as a consummate debater, joined other clubs, and began to dominate the London debating scene. In 1882, after a bout with smallpox, Shaw grew the long, pointed red beard that would be his trademark and transform him into something of a mesmeric figure.

In the Zetetical Society, Shaw met a kindred spirit whose life would intertwine with his for years to come. Sidney Webb, dwarfish in appearance and brilliant of mind, fascinated Shaw. Webb had a photographic memory, and, according to Shaw, always knew more on any given subject than did anyone else at a debate or a lecture, including the lecturer. Webb's knowledge and Shaw's style and panache were a fitting complement. The two would soon become nearly inseparable, as Shaw, with his oratorical skills, became an effective mouthpiece for Webb's brilliant ideas.

Shaw's desire to further his oratorical skills led him to attend a lecture in 1882 by the American socialist Henry George. Shaw, whose life had never been particularly good under the current capitalist society, was a willing listener. The lecture transformed his social ideology, and sent him to seek out those who believed, like him, in the tenets of socialism. In this way, Shaw came, inevitably, to read the masterwork of the socialist movement, Karl Marx's *Das Kapital.* Though Shaw would come to disagree with many of the particular economic points made by the German Marx, reading *Das Kapital* lent a new maturity to the young socialist's philosophy: "Marx made a man of me," Shaw would later assert.

Also in the reading room of the British Museum Shaw met the drama critic William Archer, who was fascinated by the young Irishman. The two began a lifelong friendship that had the immediate advantage of gaining Shaw work, at first as a book reviewer, then as an art critic. As usual, Shaw was at best blunt, often harsh, and even outrageous in his reviews, and he drew much public attention. His success as a critic led to more highly visible positions over the next two decades as a music critic and ultimately as a theater critic for the *Saturday Review.*

In his role as a critic, Shaw became a significant voice in the London artistic scene. He aspired to become a political force as well. In 1884 Shaw and Sidney Webb joined the newly founded Fabian Society. The Fabians dedicated themselves to promoting socialism, the belief that wealth and power should be shared by all members of society. Shaw was soon writing pamphlets and lecturing on socialist issues for the Fabians. He advocated socialist causes with unmatched zeal: "I spoke in the streets, in the parks, at demonstrations, anywhere and everywhere possible," he said. The contemporary writer Kingsley Martin expressed his admiration of Shaw the orator:

> He [Shaw] made an indelible impression on me at this first meeting. I cannot recall what he spoke about. It mattered little. It was George Bernard Shaw you remembered; his physical magnificence, splendid bearing, superb elocution, unexpected Irish brogue, and continuous wit were the chief memories of his speech. He would give his nose a thoughtful twitch between his thumb and finger while the audience laughed. He was one of the best speakers I ever heard.

Shaw's and Webb's combined gifts helped elevate the Fabians to a prominent position in English politics. In addition to lecturing, Shaw wrote numerous essays aimed at educating the general public about Fabian ideas. During the coming years the Fabians gained influence over the liberal British Labour Party and even helped elect members of Parliament.

BECOMING A PLAYWRIGHT

Shaw's friendship with William Archer had one other effect that proved even more important than his gaining employment as a critic. When the two decided that Shaw's weakness in constructing plots was Archer's strength, and Archer's weakness in dialogue and characterization was Shaw's forte, they decided to collaborate on a play. But the partnership was short-lived. In writing the play that would become *Widower's Houses*, Shaw declined to use Archer's plot in the entire first act. When he did address Archer's story line in act 2, he found that he exhausted it after only a few pages. Shaw completed the play, which dealt with the topic of slum landlords, eight years later in 1892, when it was finally staged.

Shaw followed *Widower's Houses* with a second play, *The Philanderer*, written in 1893. *The Philanderer* was semiautobiographical, based on a series of flirtations with women that Shaw, who fancied himself something of a ladies' man, had pursued in the 1880s. The play dealt with the power struggle between men and women in a much more provocative manner than had previously been shown on the stage.

But Shaw found it almost impossible to get his plays produced, primarily because he was writing in defiance of longstanding doctrines that had dominated the English stage for the entire Victorian era. The dominant mode, the so-called well-made play championed by such playwrights as Victorien Sardou and the Frenchman Eugene Scribe, called for highly melodramatic and unrealistic plots.

Shaw was disdainful of the cheap sensationalism of such dramas. As a Fabian socialist, he wanted art not just to entertain, but to instruct his audience in the proper way to live in a complex, changing society. Just as he loved to debate current social issues, he wrote plays that critiqued and debated English culture. His third play, *Mrs. Warren's Profession*, written in 1893, treated the subject of prostitution as the natural outgrowth of English capitalism. It could not, of course, be produced in prim and proper Victorian England. Even when it was performed in New York, its scandalous subject matter proved disastrous. As Shaw himself described the scene, "all the worst elements in the New York population came in enormous crowds. There were almost riots outside the theatre, and fabulous prices were paid for seats. The police then went in and arrested the entire company."

Having aroused public notoriety rather than gained appreciation with his treatment of controversial subjects, Shaw moved from these early plays, which he labeled "Plays Unpleasant," to a period of writing "Plays Pleasant." Though the tone of the plays that followed was less bitter and caustic than that in his previous works, Shaw continued to treat serious issues of the day. In 1894 he completed *Arms and the Man*, a satire of modern warfare, and soon after, *Candida*, which, like Ibsen's *A Doll's House*, dealt with a woman's dissatisfaction in her marriage. *Arms and the Man* opened in April 1894. It was generally well received, but its light-hearted treatment of war angered many, including the prince of Wales, who believed it to be the work of a madman.

Due to his early inability to find producers for his plays, he took to publishing them in book form. Along with the script of the play, he often added long prefaces and afterwords, and his stage directions were far longer and more descriptive than those of other playwrights. In this manner, Shaw developed an entirely new form of drama, in which the play of ideas was often more important than plot and characterization.

In 1898, Shaw married Charlotte Payne-Townsend, an Irish millionaire who was also a Fabian. This marriage would endure until Charlotte's death in 1943. Charlotte had nursed Shaw back to health following an illness that nearly killed him. He was forty-two and she forty when they married, and if there was little passion in the marriage, there was much devotion. In many ways Charlotte filled the role of a caring, nurturing mother that Bessie Shaw never could. The marriage also had the effect of making Shaw independently wealthy.

After his marriage, Shaw resigned from his post as a theater critic. Despite his limited success on the stage, he now concentrated on writing for the theater instead of about it, and entered into his most productive period as a playwright. His popularity grew even though he never abandoned his penchant for making his audiences confront the unpleasant realities of everyday life. Shaw followed his early efforts with a one-act, *The Man of Destiny*, written in 1895 and performed in 1897; *You Never Can Tell*, written in 1896 and performed in 1899; *The Devil's Disciple* (written in 1896 and performed in 1897); *Caesar and Cleopatra* (written in 1898 and performed in 1901); and *Captain Brassbound's Conversion* (written in 1899 and performed in 1900). Though he gained a wider English audience, his greatest success during this period came abroad, where *The Devil's Disciple* played to New York audiences who were more receptive to Shaw's biting satire and controversial subject matter.

A SUCCESSFUL PLAYWRIGHT

Not until 1904, when Harley Granville Barker, a young actor, director, and playwright, assumed management of the Court Theatre in London, was Shaw's work regularly produced for the English stage. Barker's theater promoted experimental work in particular, specializing in new and progressive drama. Shaw began writing new plays specifically for the Court Theatre. Until the production of *Pygmalion* in 1914, every play Shaw wrote was produced either by Barker or by one of his friends at London's other experimental theaters. Four major plays highlighted the Court Theatre's Shavian offerings: with *John Bull's Other Island, Man and Superman, Major Barbara,* and *The Doctor's Dilemma,* Shaw began to gain a reputation as a major English playwright.

Shaw continued to confront important political and social issues in these plays. *John Bull's Other Island* was an often harsh representation of his birth country, Ireland, and depicted the long-standing struggle between England and Ireland. English audiences reacted favorably to this topical play, though Shaw was nearly as biting in his satire of Englishmen as he was toward the Irish. *Man and Superman* explored the theme of the great individual in society. This play was so ambitious in its philosophical themes that it required nearly eight hours to act onstage. Most subsequent productions omit a two-hour-long middle section that Shaw titled *Don Juan in Hell.* Nevertheless, *Man and Superman* has gone on to become one of Shaw's more popular plays, and *Don Juan in Hell* is often staged as a complete play in its own right.

Major Barbara contrasted charitable organizations with capitalistic corporations and sided with neither. In its contrasting portrayals of the earnest Salvation Army worker, Barbara, and her munitions building industrialist father, *Major Barbara* won many fans, including British prime minister Winston Churchill, who felt that its debate of contemporary issues represented "the very acme of modernity." In a similar manner, *The Doctor's Dilemma,* which satirized the medical profession, raised issues of medical ethics and professionalism that are still debated to this day. Shaw's plays were not only beginning to attract audiences of his contemporaries, but would prove to have remarkable staying power over the course of the twentieth century.

Each of these plays was soon published in book form, often accompanied by long philosophical prefaces and afterwords. Here Shaw's mature philosophy of life began to emerge. He did not believe in Darwinian evolution, a prevailing doctrine in late Victorian England. Instead, he envisioned an ever-evolving "life force," by which man could will himself ever upward until he achieved the status of a superman, as far removed from his present condition as he himself was removed from the apes. This was a particularly iconoclastic philosophy, devoid of conventional religion, but Shaw was never an ordinary thinker: "Beware of the man whose god is in the skies," writes Shaw's character John Tanner in "The Revolutionist's Handbook," a prose section appended to *Man and Superman.*

Success bred success for Shaw. He continued to produce plays at the rate of almost one per year. These included *Getting Married* (1907–1908), *Misalliance* (1909), *Overruled* (1912), and *Androcles and the Lion* (1912).

PYGMALION

Shortly after his mother's death in 1913, Shaw began to passionately pursue what had become his great obsession, a flirtatious relationship with Mrs. Patrick Campbell, born Beatrice Stella Tanner. Shaw had had numerous opportunities to see this renowned actress, at the time perhaps second in prominence only to Ellen Terry as a female performer. With her constant companions, a series of foul-smelling, petulant lap dogs, she was a demanding presence, apparently so difficult to endure that her husband had reputedly fled to South Africa to work in the gold mines after three years of marriage. Though Shaw would court her extensively through letters, he knew better than to try to attempt any permanent relationship with her. "I would not have lasted a week," he said years later, after her death. It was not so much her acting that attracted Shaw, but her presence. As biographer Michael Holroyd writes:

> [Shaw] had seen her in many plays, never knowing what to expect. 'She creates all sort of illusions, and gives one all sorts of searching sensations,' he wrote. 'It is impossible not to feel that those haunting eyes are brooding on a momentous past, and the parting lips anticipating a thrilling imminent future. . . . Mrs. Patrick Campbell is a wonderful woman.'

As early as 1897 Shaw had considered writing a part especially for Mrs. Pat, as she was often called. In 1912 he finally began the task, and the part written especially for Mrs. Campbell was that of Eliza Doolittle. The role, with its early yowling and howling and boisterousness, both gently mocked and took full advantage of Mrs. Campbell's formidable reputation as a diva of the English stage. Shaw was quite perplexed over how to present the role of Eliza Doolittle to such a woman, but when he finally chose to do so by reading the play to her, she soon guessed Shaw's intention and readily accepted the role. Shaw had his Eliza, but his love affair with Mrs. Pat ended long before the play premiered. She grew tired of hounding him to leave his wife, and eventually ran off with another married man, George Cornwallis-West, a captain and socialite who was something of a real-life, aristocratic Freddy Eynsford Hill.

Pygmalion had already been performed to enthusiastic audiences in Germany and Austria, but the English production of *Pygmalion*, which opened on April 11, 1914, was unrivaled. Sir Herbert Tree, another famous English actor, was chosen to direct the play as well as to star as Henry Higgins. From the onset Tree was at odds with Shaw over how to play the role. In particular, he wanted to stress the romantic potential between Eliza and Higgins, something Shaw could not abide. If, as biographer Michael Holroyd has suggested, one of Shaw's chief intentions in the play was to suggest the platonic relationship between his own mother and her teacher George Vandeleur Lee, a romantic liaison between Eliza and Henry was out of the question. Shaw's fight to keep this relationship strictly business was one he would revisit with every new production of the play—both on stage and onscreen—and usually lose.

Shaw sat through the first performance almost against his own will. For him, the play was saved only by the presence of Mrs. Pat. But he could not bear to return until the one hundredth performance, and even then he was not pleased by Tree's romantic advances toward Mrs. Pat's Eliza, which included throwing flowers toward her at the end of the play. Tree was, in Shaw's words, "utterly innocent of the meaning of the play, and so pleased with himself as Eliza's lover, that he had no idea of the outrage to me."

Pygmalion continued to play to enthusiastic audiences during the spring and summer of 1914 until on June 28, a Serbian nationalist assassinated the archduke Ferdinand of Austria and World War I broke out. *Pygmalion*'s run ended shortly after, as the world that had produced such a charming play seemed to disappear.

SHAW AND THE GREAT WAR

Shaw's next literary efforts were inextricably tied to the war. He believed that "mankind must put an end to war or war will put an end to mankind." Disgusted with all of the participating countries, and holding none blameless, he voiced his unpopular opinions in a pamphlet, *Common Sense About the War*. For Shaw, World War I was nothing less than the failure of capitalism and the futile attempt of nineteenth-century empires to maintain their control. He wrote:

> I regard war as wasteful, demoralizing, unnecessary, and ludicrously and sordidly inglorious in its reality. This is my unconditional opinion. I don't mean war in a bad cause, or war against liberty, or war with any other qualification whatever: I mean war. I recognize no right of the good man to kill the bad man or to govern the bad man.

But no one wanted to hear Shaw's remarks about the futility of war or the waste of young lives. He was subsequently regarded as a pariah in his adopted country, snubbed in social and literary circles alike. The Germans even used the pamphlet as propaganda against the British, since Shaw had argued that the English were equally to blame in conducting a wasteful and shameless war. As the war dragged on, many realized that Shaw's honest analysis, free of the bias that plagued almost all wartime statements, contained common-sense rather than treasonous remarks. Shaw's reputation would recover and grow stronger than ever.

During the war, the English theater was virtually shut down. Shaw's dramatic writing dwindled to a single play, *Heartbreak House*, which he wrote in 1913, then rewrote, and which Shaw withheld from production until well after the war ended. Wartime production would probably have been impossible, for its portrait of prewar England was not flattering. The play concerned a desperate and effete people at the beginning of the twentieth century anticipating the outbreak of a great war that would be not only destructive but also cleansing. Its setting is Captain Shotover's house, which is built in the form of a ship. The setting symbolizes the modern Ship of State, in this case England. In the play's most trenchant exchange, Shotover asserts that the business of a modern-day Englishman is "navigation. Learn it and live; or leave it and be damned." The metaphor clearly refers to contemporary politics and socioeconomics in England, which in Shaw's opinion had been sailing on the wrong course for many years. Some of the characters who cannot learn "navigation" in *Heartbreak House* are killed in a bomb-ing raid, yet others call for additional bombs to finish the job. This is Shaw's Noah's Ark, a nonbiblical attempt to rid Europe of all that was wrong with the nineteenth century and begin the twentieth century purified of the evils of the past. In later years Shaw would refer to *Heartbreak House* as his best play.

TWO GREAT PLAYS

After the war, Shaw wrote two of his more highly regarded plays, which helped salvage his wounded reputation. *Back to Methuselah* was an ambitious work of five sections, each a full-length play in its own right. Perhaps Shaw's most philosophical play since *Man and Superman*, *Back to Methuselah* is an ambitious attempt to expound upon his philosophy of life and the direction in which humans should be heading. He subtitled the drama *A Metabiological Penta-teuch*, referring to the first five books of the Old Testament, as he investigated his own religion of the life force and its inevitable uplifting of the human race. The play's setting reaches from the mythical creation of man and woman in the Garden of Eden to the eventual disembodiment of humans in the year 31920. In this far-off future, humans are virtually immortal. The have no bodies and depend solely on the intellect for pleasure.

This impractical theatrical gesture was far too long to be performed in a single evening, and, like John Milton's epic tale of creation and the fall of man, *Paradise Lost*, it would demand "fit audience . . . though few." The story goes that when producer Barry Jackson requested that Shaw allow him to stage the play in Birmingham, England, the playwright asked if Jackson had already provided for the financial well-being of his wife and children. Shaw's implication was that any production of *Back to Methuselah* would surely not be a moneymaker. Jackson's production divided the play into four parts, to be played on successive nights. Shaw was mightily impressed by Jackson's fortitude and pleased with the performance. To show his appreciation, after the play's conclusion Shaw not only answered calls of "Author!" with a short speech, but launched into an impromptu dance onstage. Since that first performance, which Shaw called "the most extraordinary experience of my life," *Back to Methuselah* has enjoyed many successful runs.

Shaw followed *Back to Methuselah* with a less ambitious but even more highly regarded effort. He had been looking for a world figure about whom to write a play. After some hesitation, he accepted the challenge of his wife, Charlotte, to chronicle the life of Joan of Arc, the martyred Frenchwoman who led troops into battle and who had been declared a saint only a few years before. Thus was the play *Saint Joan* born. Shaw had always been known for his comic worldview in plays such as *Pygmalion*, even when he was tackling difficult and profound topics. *Saint Joan* was as close to tragedy as Shaw would come. In his depiction of the brave struggle of one woman against both church and state, Shaw created a true hero in Joan of Arc. Many critics regard *Saint Joan* as Shaw's masterpiece.

INTERNATIONAL FAME

George Bernard Shaw's fame had now spread far and wide. He was besieged by offers of prizes and awards that come with the recognition of literary greatness. As Sally Peters writes, "He had achieved an unprecedented international celebrity, unsurpassed even by the great religious and political leaders. His every word was recorded, his every movement publicized." Shaw turned down most of the awards that were offered to him, having no need for literary prizes. "They eat up money; elicit a lot of trash; and invariably go to some second best composition. You cannot give examination paper marks to works of art," he said in his characteristically sardonic manner. Shaw reputedly even turned down the offer of a knighthood that would have made him Sir George Bernard Shaw. But one award was too prestigious to refuse: In 1925, Shaw was awarded the Nobel Prize in literature. Nevertheless, Shaw did not accept the prize money for himself. He arranged for the money to be used to translate Swedish works of literature into English.

As Shaw passed his seventieth birthday, his best dramatic works were behind him. An elderly figure with white hair and a white beard, he would yet live almost another quarter of a century. Shaw continued to write, considering himself, as he once said, a "writing machine." His play *The Apple Cart*, produced in 1929, had a successful run in London. In the play, Shaw imagined a strikingly Shavian king of England and used the plot as a vehicle to comment on numerous contemporary British issues, including politics, systems of government, religion, and leadership.

Given his fame and success, it was not surprising that film producers clamored for the rights to his plays. After all, theater was the literary genre most easily adapted to the emerging art form of cinema. But Shaw was greatly dissatisfied with the movie industry. He did not want his words or his scenes altered, and to fit the screen format, directors often wanted to take great liberties with his plays. Shaw's *Arms and the Man* had been made into an operetta, *The Chocolate Soldier*, which Shaw considered an abomination. When a film of the same name was proposed, he filed suit to stop it. The experience of seeing others mishandle his work almost convinced him to never allow his work to be adapted. Nevertheless, in 1937, the producer Gabriel Pascal convinced Shaw to let *Pygmalion* be turned into a movie, for which Shaw himself would write the screenplay. Shaw, never easy to work with, at first told Pascal that he should go to Covent Garden in London and pick the first flower girl he saw to play the role of Eliza. But a less flippant Shaw was more helpful in bringing his play to the screen. In 1938, he became the only Nobel laureate to also win an Oscar when his screenplay for *Pygmalion* was so honored.

In 1947, at ninety-two years of age, Shaw wrote: "I cannot hold my tongue nor my pen. As long as I live I must write. If I stopped writing I should die for wanting something to do." He spent most of his time at his longtime home in Ayot St. Lawrence. Piles of letters would arrive at his door, requesting everything from autographs to personal appearances and speaking engagements. The sheer mass of requests forced Shaw to turn down almost all of them. In September 1950, while pruning a tree in his garden, George Bernard Shaw slipped and fell. He was rescued by servants, but suffered a fractured thigh, from which he never recovered. He died on November 2, 1950, at the age of ninety-four.

Characters and Plot

Henry Higgins: A professor of linguistics, Henry Higgins is as rude and ungracious in polite society as he is refined and precise in the study of language. He speaks in the most civilized of accents and dresses impeccably, but he has little use for polite society and its pretensions. He can be boorish and unthinking in his behavior toward others, and he treats most people as simply part of his experiments. He is also a braggart, but he can back up his claims with his superior abilities.

Eliza Doolittle: A common, lower-class girl who sells flowers on the streets of London, Eliza has tremendous willpower and hidden abilities. Despite her coarse appearance, she is also a woman of great tenderness and caring, who more than anything wants to please and be loved. She undergoes a miraculous transformation from flower girl to high-society lady, but once she has arrived, she has little understanding of what to do with herself.

Colonel Pickering: The foil to Higgins, Pickering is a man of impressive abilities who also has a heart. As the author of *Spoken Sanskrit,* he has the intellectual stature to engage Higgins on his own level. He cares deeply for Eliza's wellbeing, even while he becomes so engaged in Higgins's scheme that he sometimes, like Higgins, seems to be playing with a human doll. Pickering conducts himself with exquisite manners; as such, he is a marked contrast to the often boorish Henry Higgins.

Freddy Eynsford Hill: A dapper young gentleman of proper stature in society but with no apparent income or the ability to earn one, Freddy falls in love at first sight with the newly polished flower girl Eliza. When Eliza leaves Higgins's home, it is the impoverished Freddy, mooning after her and waiting outside the house, who sets off with her in a taxi—using Eliza's money. In Shaw's "sequel" to *Pygmalion,* in order to end the hue and cry for a romantic ending from theatergoers, he suggests that Eliza marries Freddy.

Mrs. Eynsford Hill: A proper English lady raising her son and daughter on virtually no income at all.

Clara Eynsford Hill: Freddy's sister, raised in "genteel poverty," she is status conscious, superficial, and eager to adopt any new fad that comes along. This is evidenced in her unhesitating willingness to adopt Eliza's "new small talk" and the improper language that seems new and daring.

Nepommuck: Higgins's former pupil is now supposedly an expert on languages, though his mentor has nothing but disdain for him and his abilities. Nepommuck falsely surmises that Eliza is a Hungarian princess, thus winning the bet for Higgins at the end of act 3 of the play. Toward the end of the play, Eliza attempts to rile Higgins by suggesting that she will become Nepommuck's assistant after parting company with him.

Mrs. Higgins: Henry's mother is a proper, upper-class lady who is often embarrassed by the antics of her famous son. She is also kind-hearted and commonsensical, and she is therefore concerned about the experiment that Higgins and Pickering are conducting on Eliza. She compares them to two little boys playing with a doll and sides with Eliza against her son when Eliza leaves Higgins and hides out at Mrs. Higgins's house.

Alfred Doolittle: Eliza's father, he is one of the more entertaining characters in literature. Initially a carefree, shiftless, ill-equipped father and husband, he is mostly interested in leisure and liquor. But his homespun philosophy amuses Henry Higgins, who obtains a substantial income for Doolittle from an American philanthropist. Once thrust into the middle class and the morality that accompanies such a position in society, Doolittle is reluctantly and amusingly forced to act the part by marrying his live-in lover and by giving up his hedonistic ways.

Mrs. Pearce: Higgins's housekeeper, she is a somewhat reluctant participant in the professor's experiment. She can be both harsh and gentle with Eliza. Although she is willing to follow Higgins's plan to transform Eliza, she objects to the harshness with which he treats the former flower girl.

PLOT SUMMARY

It is 11:15 P.M. in London's Covent Garden. The theater has let out just as a violent storm arises, and a group of theatergoers has taken shelter under the portico of St. Paul's Church. Everyone in the crowd looks anxiously out at the rain except for one man, his back turned to the others, who scribbles in a notebook. He, we will learn, is Professor Henry Higgins.

Freddy Eynsford Hill has been sent by his mother and his sister to hail a cab. He returns unsuccessfully and, after receiving criticism from mother and sister, starts out again only to crash into Eliza Doolittle, a poor young woman with a strong Cockney accent who has been trying to sell flowers to the crowd. When Eliza calls Freddy by name, "Watch where you're going, Freddy," the young man's mother demands to know how such a poor wench knows her son's name. But after paying for the flowers ruined in the accident with Freddy, Mrs. Eynsford Hill is informed by Eliza that it was only a random guess.

Colonel Pickering, an elderly gentleman, seeks shelter under the same building. When Eliza asks him to buy a flower, he says he does not have the change; instead, he gives her three hapence (half pennies) from his pocket. When a stranger informs Eliza that a man in the crowd has been writing down every word she says, she begins to protest that she is a good girl. Henry Higgins steps to the forefront, and he soon amazes the crowd with his uncanny ability to tell their hometown based on their speech patterns. Several in the crowd, including Freddy's sister, are offended by such an upstart, and others wonder if he is a police informer. When Pickering questions whether there is a living to be made through Higgins's talent, Higgins informs him that many a man of humble origins will pay handsomely to have a lower-class accent refined. In fact, Higgins boasts, if he worked with Eliza, he could pass her off as a duchess within three months.

The two men then introduce themselves and realize that each has been seeking out the other. Higgins is the author of *Higgins's Universal Alphabet* and Pickering of *Spoken Sanskrit.* By now the rain has ceased, and Freddy's mother and sister decide to walk to the station. As they start off together, Eliza asks if Higgins will buy a flower. After an exchange of insults, Higgins flings a pocketful of change at her. Freddy arrives with a cab only to learn that his mother and sister have left, and Eliza uses her windfall from Higgins to ride home in style in the cab.

The next day, at Henry Higgins's home on fashionable Wimpole Street, Higgins and Pickering spend the morning in the laboratory listening to sounds. Higgins uses his elaborate array of sound machines while attempting to teach Pickering to differentiate between subtle vowel sounds. At 11:00 A.M., as Pickering grows weary of the exercises, the servant Mrs. Pearce announces a female. When Higgins discovers it is Eliza, his hope of hearing a new accent is dashed and he wants to send her away immediately. But Eliza insists that she has a proposition for him: He can earn back some of the money he threw at her the previous evening by giving her pronunciation lessons. Higgins has a good laugh over this absurdity, but Eliza insists that she wants to learn to speak in a more refined tongue so that she may be able to work in a flower shop. When Pickering reminds Higgins of his boast the previous evening and offers to pay for Eliza's lessons, the wager is on. Higgins will attempt to make Eliza into a lady who can pass for royalty. Mrs. Pearce takes Eliza upstairs for a bath and a makeover, but Eliza balks at having to disrobe, claiming she is a "good girl." Mrs. Pearce scoffs at Eliza's silliness and forces her to clean herself thoroughly so that she may be presentable and not exude an unpleasant odor in the company of the gentlemen.

Mrs. Pearce returns downstairs after bathing Eliza and makes several requests of Henry Higgins. She asks that he be more gentle in his actions with Eliza, who is not used to his harshness, as is Mrs. Pearce. She asks that he refrain from swearing, which, at the time, means avoiding phrases such as "what the devil." Higgins is shocked to realize that he is not the model of decorum he believes himself to be, but he agrees to mend his ways.

Mr. Alfred Doolittle, a common dustman (garbage collector) is announced. He enters, and informs Higgins and Pickering that they have his daughter in the house. Adopting his usual uncaring and confrontational posture, Higgins suggests the dustman take his daughter at once. But Doolittle does not want his daughter back. He wants only five pounds, enough money to get drunk on. When the men question whether Doolittle would actually sell his daughter, Doolittle responds that he cannot afford morals. By his own admission he is one of the "undeserving poor." Doolittle expounds on his position in society, his lack of morality, and his lifestyle until Higgins and Pickering are positively amused by this witty rascal. Higgins wants to give him ten pounds, but Doolittle will only take five. Eliza comes downstairs. Dressed in a blue cotton kimono imprinted with small white jasmines, she appears "dainty and exquisitely clean," so that Doolittle does not recognize her at first. He states that her cleaning up so well is a credit to the family, takes his five pounds, and leaves.

We next see a sample of Eliza Doolittle's speech lessons. Higgins, rude and peremptory as always, badgers Eliza to concentrate more on pronouncing her letters correctly, beginning with *A, B, C,* which Eliza renders as *Ahyee, Buh yee, Cuh yee.* Despite her small success in saying *cup* correctly, Eliza finds it difficult to satisfy the demanding Higgins and runs crying from the room.

Months have passed when Henry Higgins shows up at his mother's house on the day she receives her visitors. He barges in rudely, as usual, and informs her of Eliza and how quickly the young former flower girl has learned her lessons. Mrs. Higgins is distressed that Henry has shown up on her "at-home" day because his condescending and inappropriate manner always embarrasses her before her guests. Today is no different. Higgins immediately senses by their accents that he has met his mother's visitors before, and he has—at Covent Garden on the same night that he first met Eliza. Mrs. Higgins's guests are the Eynsford Hills: mother, daughter, and son, Freddy.

Higgins engages in some rather rude small talk with the Eynsford Hills, mixing in an occasional swear word. It is clear that he has no conception of how to conduct himself in society and little patience for polite talk. Colonel Pickering arrives with Eliza, who is presented before the group. She is dazzling to look at, and her speech is perfect, even royal. She has been informed that she must keep to two topics: the weather and everybody's health. Eliza first discusses the weather with the precision of a meteorologist, which amuses Freddy in particular. He is quite evidently enamored of the beautiful young woman. But when Eliza tells a story about the ill health of her aunt, whom she believes to have been "done in," or murdered, by unscrupulous relatives, the weakness in Henry's training becomes clear. He has only taught the correct form for high-society speech and not the content. Henry tries to pass off her inappropriate content and jarring mixture of high language and low colloquialisms as the new small talk. Before Eliza can launch into another speech, Henry loudly clears his throat, which is the signal for her to depart. The Eynsford Hills are all charmed by Eliza and her new small talk. When Freddy asks if she is walking home in order to ascertain if he may accompany her, Eliza demurs, saying, "Walk. Not bloody likely. I am going in a taxi." *Bloody* is a notorious English swear word, and the remark causes a sensation, yet it is soon accepted by those present as another element of the new small talk.

After the Eynsford Hills have left, Mrs. Higgins scolds Pickering and her son, calling them "a pretty pair of babies," playing with a "live doll." But Henry and the colonel are giddy with their limited success with Eliza. They spend all of their time, they say, working with Eliza, dressing Eliza, listening to Eliza's witticisms. When Mrs. Higgins questions the propriety of a single woman living with two men, they are similarly unconcerned. Their lives now revolve around preparing Eliza to pass for a duchess. Mrs. Higgins raises another issue: What is to be done with Eliza once the men's scheme is complete. Again, Higgins is unconcerned. He will find her some "light employment."

More time has passed as Henry and Pickering prepare Eliza for the final test. They take her to an embassy ball in London, where she is presented before high society, including the ambassador and his wife. Among the group is a man who claims to be Henry Higgins's first pupil, his "best and greatest pupil," who has made Higgins's name famous throughout Europe. Nepommuck is an interpreter who can speak thirty-two languages and sniff out an imposter with ease. But he cannot expose Eliza. Applying all of his linguistic knowledge, Nepommuck declares the strange young woman to be a Hungarian princess, for she speaks English too well, as only those who have been taught it as a foreign language can. When Higgins asks if Nepommuck has spoken to Eliza in Hungarian, he replies that he has, and that she had cleverly answered, "Please speak to me in English: I do not understand French." Higgins then declares that Miss Doolittle strikes him as a common flower girl from Drury Lane, but the others all scoff at the suggestion as preposterous.

Higgins has won his bet, and the triumphant trio, exhausted from their efforts, leave the party. Once at home,

Pickering and Higgins boisterously celebrate their triumph as Eliza hovers in the background. As Pickering goes off to bed, Higgins prepares to do the same, wondering aloud where his slippers are. Eliza steps forward and throws them at the nonplussed Higgins. He cannot fathom why she is upset, but Eliza is enraged that her part in winning the bet has not been acknowledged. Even more important, she is worried about her future. What will she do now that the men no longer need her? Eliza and Higgins argue heatedly, and the battle stops just short of becoming physical. Higgins believes that Eliza is not duly grateful to him for rescuing her from the streets, while Eliza feels unwanted and afraid. Threatening to leave the house, Eliza asks Higgins if the clothes she has worn are her own, for she does not want to be accused of stealing. Henry is supremely offended. As the argument reaches its climax, he declares that he does not give a damn about anything, including Eliza. Calling her a "heartless guttersnipe," he storms off to bed.

Eliza goes to her room, packs a bag, and leaves the house. Outside she is surprised to find the lovelorn Freddy Eynsford Hill, who informs her that he waits outside the house on Wimpole Street almost every night. "It's the only place where I'm happy," he remarks. The two smother each other in kisses until a constable (police officer) interrupts them. When the constable leaves, they embrace again, but a second constable puts an end to their public display. Eliza wants to rent a passing taxi, but Freddy has no money. Ironically, Eliza does, for one of Colonel Pickering's rules is to never leave the house without at least ten pounds. Eliza and Freddy plan to spend the night riding around London. In the morning, she will seek the aid of Henry's mother, the venerable Mrs. Higgins.

The next morning a frantic Higgins and Pickering show up at Mrs. Higgins's house. They have been searching for Eliza and have even notified the police. As Mrs. Higgins attempts to talk some sense into the two, a gentleman visitor named Mr. Doolittle is announced. The man turns out to be the same Alfred Doolittle, Eliza's father, whom they had met at Wimpole Street—with one great difference. As a lark, Higgins had given an aging American millionaire philanthropist Doolittle's name, claiming Alfred as the most original moralist England had to offer. Upon the American's death, he had willed Doolittle "four thousand a year," plunging the poor man into the depths of middle-class morality and respectability, which he had consciously avoided. He blames Higgins for perpetrating this offense on him. When Mrs. Higgins points out that he can always reject the money, Doolittle replies that he has not the nerve. He is intimidated, he says.

Now that Alfred can support his daughter, the question of Eliza's future seems for the moment a nonissue, but Doolittle already has more dependent relatives than he knows what to do with and Higgins wants Eliza back.

Asking Higgins to maintain his best behavior, and Alfred to step out of the room so as not to shock Eliza all at once, Mrs. Higgins requests the young woman's presence. Eliza greets Higgins with cold courtesy and does not react to his order to "get up and come home." She is warmer toward Pickering, who, she says, has taught her the most about being a lady through the kind and respectful manner in which he has always treated her.

Alfred Doolittle returns to the room, shocking Eliza. He reveals that he is to be married to Eliza's stepmother that very day, and Mrs. Higgins, Pickering and Eliza all offer to attend. As they prepare for this event, Higgins and Eliza are left alone. A long conversation ensues, in which they display friendship, anger, tenderness, and a range of other emotions toward each other. Between calling her a fool and an idiot and even a "damned impudent slut," in his usual unfeeling manner, Higgins several times asks Eliza to return to Wimpole Street as a pal, of sorts, so that they may live like "three old bachelors." But Eliza demands what Higgins can never give: a display of genuine caring for her. She takes leave of him, having informed him of her plan to marry Freddy Eynsford Hill. This eventuality strikes Higgins as absurd, and the play ends with him roaring with laughter over the possibility.

CHAPTER 1

Background on *Pygmalion*

READINGS ON
PYGMALION

The Origin of
Pygmalion

Richard Huggett

Richard Huggett recounts the story of how George Bernard Shaw came to write *Pygmalion* for the renowned stage actress Mrs. Stella Patrick Campbell, one of the most talented, beautiful, and difficult actresses of her day. Such was her stage presence, and so infatuated with her would Shaw become, that the part of Eliza was written with Campbell specifically in mind. But how could Shaw convince a notorious diva to play the part of an obnoxious-sounding, poverty-ridden guttersnipe? Huggett tells of the meeting between the playwright and the actress, arranged by a mutual friend, during which Shaw first read the script of *Pygmalion* to Campbell—who then agreed to play Eliza. Huggett is the author of *Supernatural on Stage: Ghosts and Superstitions of the Theatre, The Truth About Pygmalion,* and the play *The First Night of Pygmalion.*

The part of Eliza Doolittle was inspired by Mrs. Patrick Campbell and written specially for her; since she is the focal point of this story, it is necessary to examine in some detail the background and personality of this extraordinary woman. She was a phenomenon, and it is unlikely that theatrical history can produce anybody who was as dazzlingly gifted in so many different ways. She was beautiful with a blazingly dark-eyed, broodingly sexual beauty which aroused poets, painters and writers to a frenzy. Her acting ability was exceptional, amounting on occasions to genius which placed her overnight at the very top of her profession in an age already filled with great actresses—Ellen Terry, Duse, Réjane and Sarah Bernhardt were pleased to accept her as their equal. Her voice was warm, rich and deep like a

Excerpted from *The Truth About Pygmalion,* by Richard Huggett (New York: Random House, 1969). Copyright © 1969 by Richard Huggett.

cello, and although there are, unhappily, no records of it, there is abundant testimony to its thrilling and hypnotic quality; when old people speak mistily of her, it is her voice they remember first. 'You make an ugly language sound beautiful,' said [French actor Benoît-Constant] Coquelin to her after he had seen her Ophelia [in Shakespeare's *Hamlet*]. If Bernhardt's voice was likened to gold, then Mrs. Pat's was purple and crimson flecked with silver. She was devastatingly witty in a period of history which was already filled with wits: her sayings were widely quoted, found their way into print and are now accepted as classics of their kind; she could even outshine Shaw and not many people were able to do that. She had a fascination and charm which was irresistible when she chose to exert it, and if all this wasn't enough, she could play the piano beautifully. She could have had a strikingly successful career as a concert pianist if she had chosen, and England's subsequent musical history might have been suitably enriched: but she chose otherwise, and music's loss was the theatre's gain. All in all, she was an arch-enchantress of a very rare and special sort, who fascinated her public and enslaved some of the greatest geniuses of her day. For the most part they went quietly, for no man could stand up to her for long if she chose to capture him.

She was born Beatrice Stella Tanner in 1865 of very mixed parentage. She was Italian on her mother's side, descended from a long line of minor and impoverished aristocracy, though her grandfather had actually descended to managing a circus and her mother to riding a horse in it. On her father's side she was English with a strong association with the Protestant clergy. The Tanners had provided the Church of England with a praiseworthy selection of vicars, deans, canons and even a bishop or two. She was an odd mixture—part Venice [Italy], part suburban Dulwich [England]. From the sun-drenched south, she derived her looks and the passionate impulsiveness of a wayward and unpredictable temperament, and from the cold north, she inherited an instinctive respectability and a strong streak of puritanism. . . .

A Difficult Actress

She started her professional career in 1888 at the age of twenty-five. Five years of hard, rigorous touring in the provinces followed and then in 1893 her sensational début at the St. James's Theatre under George Alexander's management in [English playwright Arthur Wing] Pinero's *The Second Mrs. Tanqueray.* History was made, and she was a super-star, long before the term was invented. Naturally she had to behave like one, and for her this meant only one thing. No sooner had she read her notices, each one a love letter from the critics, than she started to assert herself in ways which few could forgive but which all were forced to tolerate. Stories began to circulate of her rudeness, her arrogance, her unreliability, her difficult conduct off the stage and her truly appalling behaviour on it. She became professionally such a nuisance that nobody who had ever been associated with her wished to repeat the experience if he could possibly avoid it. What was this imp of perversity which made her behave so badly so soon after her name was made? Somewhere deep down in that strangely complex personality was a terrifying instability, an almost suicidal neurosis which forced her to try and destroy what she had so carefully created. But try as she might, even she could not destroy such a brilliant career because for twenty years, while she was in her prime, she was unique and irreplaceable, and the theatre has always secretly loved its bitch-goddesses. She could behave as she did with impunity; she knew it and so did everybody else. Even George Alexander, a pompous, self-important, humourless man who was her chief victim, was compelled to offer her no less than six engagements, though each time the wretched, persecuted man swore it would be the last. . . .

SHAW MEETS MRS. PAT

On that first glorious night at the St James's Theatre in 1803 it was tears, cheers, roses and champagne—and Bernard Shaw. This is where the story really starts, for he was in the audience. Hers was, by all accounts, one of the most sensational débuts of the twentieth century. Nobody remotely like her had been seen before or was to be seen again. Not only had she put on the stage a new sort of woman, but she had almost succeeded in convincing the critics that Pinero had written a new sort of play. Only Shaw seemed to have realized that he hadn't—the model was fully sixty years old and dying on its feet, but Pinero, with the cunning of a veteran craftsman, had neatly disguised the fact. Shaw was enraptured with her, but it is typical of him that he should have announced that it was her piano playing and her physical dexterity which had impressed him most. 'She's unique,' he remarked to Pinero, 'not that she's a great actress, *but she can thread a needle with her toes!*' This must be taken with a large pinch of Shavian salt, for contradicting himself was a favourite hobby amounting to an occupational disease, which caused bewilderment to his contemporaries and confusion to his biographers. Whatever he said or wrote about Mrs. Pat, the fact remained that Shaw had the greatest possible respect for her acting abilities. During his three-year tenure as dramatic critic for *The Saturday Review,* he lavished the most eloquent praise on her best performances, and as further proof of his sincerity, when he started to write plays in 1892, he wanted her for many of his leading parts.

THE SOURCES OF *PYGMALION*

Suggestions abound regarding the sources of Shaw's inspiration for Pygmalion. *The play bears a remarkable resemblance to the popular eighteenth-century English novel* Humphrey Clinker *by Tobias Smollett.*

In . . . 1912, [Shaw] wrote *Pygmalion,* the idea for which had been buzzing round his head for fifteen years, for he wrote to [actress and friend] Ellen Terry about it in 1897—even then he had [actress] Mrs. Patrick Campbell in mind for it. There have been many attempts at trying to trace the source of Shaw's inspiration for this play. One suggestion, made by [Shaw biographer] R.F. Rattray, is that while he was sitting in Rodin's studio in Paris for his bust by that great French sculptor, he remembered the classical legend of Pygmalion, the statue with which the sculptor had fallen in love; but that was in 1906, nine years after the idea for the play had occurred to him. Sir Barry Jackson, who was responsible some years later for the Malvern Festivals, where so many of Shaw's plays were presented, quotes the German dramatic critics as saying that Shaw actually found the plot in Tobias Smollett's novel *Humphrey Clinker.* 'The plot is so close,' says Jackson, 'that I challenged GBS [George Bernard Shaw] about it. I said: "You've been reading your Smollett." He replied: "I can't remember doing that." Then he quickly changed the subject, which he was fond of doing when he wanted to avoid being pressed further. I think he must have read *Humphrey Clinker* years ago in the British Museum and it remained tucked away in the back of his brain.'

R.J. Minney, *The Bogus Image of Bernard Shaw.* London: Leslie Frewin, 1969.

. . . In fact, Cleopatra [in *Caesar and Cleopatra*] was the only one of these which she did play, and it was a single performance in Newcastle [England] in 1899, hastily thrown together to establish the copyright.

In 1897 she joined Forbes Robertson's company at the Lyceum for a season of classical revivals. She played Ophelia to his Hamlet and Shaw noted with approval that in the mad scene she was truly, terrifyingly and astonishingly mad. Three months later he returned to see it a second time, but the production and all the performances had deteriorated badly. Mrs. Pat was now thoroughly bored with Ophelia—'a very silly girl, she needed a good shaking,' was her comment—and instead of madness, now offered the stereotyped sentimental idiocy familiar to, and favoured by, the Victorian theatregoers. None of this would be worthy of attention or comment but for one interesting fact: it was this performance which, strangely enough, gave Shaw the first idea for *Pygmalion* though it was some fifteen years before he actually came to writing it. 'Caesar and Cleopatra have been driven clean out of my head by a play I wish to write for them in which he shall be a West End gentleman and she a flower-girl with an apron and three red ostrich feathers in her hat. Oooooh, she'll be a rapscallionly flower-girl!' Just what Mrs. Pat was doing to make Shaw think of a flower-girl is not known, but apparently there was something in the way she sang and decked herself with flowers in the mad scene which reminded him irresistibly of the lady who sold flowers in Charing Cross station.

Shortly after this they were introduced to each other and proceeded to exchange their first cautious letters. 'My dear Mrs. Patrick Campbell . . .' 'Dear Mr. Shaw . . .'. . .

Fifteen years passed during which time Shaw forgot all about his flower-girl and the lady who was to inspire her. Apart from a few casual, friendly letters, he and Mrs. Pat had no communication with each other, each being busy with their separate careers. . . .

MEETING AGAIN

Then in 1912 she played one of the last of her six engagements with the long-suffering George Alexander, now Sir George and a very dignified gentleman. This was an adaptation by Robert Hichens of his own highly popular novel, *Bella Donna*, a torrid, atmospheric romantic drama set in the Far East which provided yet another display of Mrs. Pat's extraordinary ability to transform a thoroughly bad play into a hugely popular success. . . .

Shaw went to see the play and in the interval paid Mrs. Pat a visit backstage. It was a long-accepted tradition in the Victorian theatre for stars to receive visitors in the interval, a custom which was accepted much more readily than it is now. In those days, because the scenery was so elaborate and required such frequent changing, the intervals were much longer. When Mrs. Pat held court in her dressing-room, intervals were liable to be very long indeed; for her convenience, the play might be cut but never the intervals. While she was changing her costume they talked about the play. 'I hate it,' she moaned, 'it's so *crude!* Bella Donna is such a bad woman. People think I'm like that, even darling Robert Hichens does. I want to play nothing but *saints,* but they won't let me. Oh, she's an abominable woman.'

'Very appropriate,' said Shaw, *'Bella Donna is* an abominable play. I've never seen anything like it. If [French playwright Victorien] Sardou and [American playwright] David Belasco had collaborated they might conceivably produce something like this. The only thing to be done with it is to set it to music. Somebody ought to invite [Italian operatic composer] Puccini. However, you're the only actress in London who could make sense out of it; it's certainly a pleasure to hear a beautiful voice. How did you get it, I've often wondered?'

'God gave it to me,' she replied smiling.

'I have only one criticism. You speak English better than anyone else in the English theatre, but it is too careful. I repeatedly find myself listening to the voice and not to the words. That may be all right for Patti but it really won't do for Mrs. Pat who's worth ten of her.'

Pygmalion Is Born

Mrs. Pat was not slow to accept this challenge. 'Will you write a play for me? Will you write your *next* play for me?' Shaw agreed. 'Then write me a cockney part,' she said with a touch of defiance, 'and I'll show you what I can do. I'm much more versatile than people suspect. I'm so tired of playing ladies. Give me something nice and common, there's a dear.' Shaw nodded and went to see Alexander who was evidently thinking along the same lines as his leading lady.

'Why don't you write a play for me, Mr. Shaw?' he said. *'Bella Donna* won't last for ever and I really do need a new play for the autumn.'

It had been a fateful day, for out of those two short conversations, *Pygmalion* was born. Shaw was a very quick worker and within a month the play was complete. . . .

HOW TO READ *PYGMALION* TO MRS. PAT

Shaw called at the St. James's Theatre and, as was his custom, read the play aloud to Alexander, his wife and his advisors. Shaw was a superb actor and he read his own plays magnificently, far better than many professional actors, which was sometimes inclined to have a discouraging effect on their performances. Alexander was not in the least discouraged: he was radiantly, boundlessly, hugely delighted. 'It's a cert, a dead cert,' he shouted. Then his face fell into unusually hard and determined lines. 'Now listen to me, Mr. Shaw,' he said, 'I'll get you any actress you like to play Eliza and I'll pay her any salary she asks, you can settle your own terms. But go on for another play with Mrs. Campbell, I will NOT!! I'd rather die.'

She was behaving very badly just then, much worse than usual. She had recently started the abominable habit of actually laughing outright on the stage during Alexander's scenes. . . . At that point Shaw had no strong views on the casting of Professor Higgins, but there was simply no question of anybody else in the West End playing Eliza. He had promised his next play to Mrs. Pat, he had given his word, and whatever his other shortcomings might be, Shaw always kept his promises. When all was said and done, he was a gentleman.

It was this decision which now placed a curious diplomatic problem in his hands. Somehow he had to acquaint Mrs. Pat with the play and obtain her approval of the part. But how? He realized that when she had expressed a desire to play a cockney part, what she had in mind was something rather genteel like Madame Sans-Gêne, the laundress who had been Ellen Terry's solitary excursion into the lower orders; or perhaps a lady's maid or shop assistant like the parts which Nancy Price was then playing so successfully, something well-dressed and clean which involved only the slightest distortion of those beautiful vowel sounds. But a flower-girl, a guttersnipe with a dreadful accent which you could hardly understand, using the most disgusting language never before heard on the stage, dirty with a lifetime's accumulated grime, crawling with fleas, and wearing rags so filthy that they had to be burned, never in her wildest dreams could she have anticipated this. How could he offer it to her with the explanation that, being a splendid ladies' tailor, the part fitted her as closely as Lady Cicely in *Captain Brassbound's Conversion* fitted Ellen Terry? Mrs. Pat was a grand lady and accustomed to very grand parts; her rages were well known to be truly terrifying and even Shaw's courage failed him at the prospect. 'I simply didn't dare offer it to her,' he wailed to Ellen Terry. But a solution presented itself; the Hon. Mrs. Edith Lyttleton, a close friend of theirs, known to them both as D.D., offered her services. Let Shaw read it to her, and let it be cunningly contrived that Mrs. Pat should also be present, so that hearing the play should seem to be by mere chance.

'There's no point in my giving her the play to read for herself,' he said irritably. 'She doesn't know how to read a play, no actress does. She'll just look at her part and ignore the rest, I *know,* and that would be the end. No, the only chance we have is to get her interested in the play as a whole and then she'll beg to play Eliza. You'll see.'

READING THE PLAY

It was quickly arranged. Mrs. Lyttleton invited both of them to tea at her house at 16 Great College Street, Westminster; the date was June 26th and it was a fine summer's day. Mrs. Pat arrived after a matinée at the theatre, 'reeking from *Bella Donna*', and full of backstage gossip. Conversation over the teacups tinkled along merrily until Mrs. Pat noticed the manuscript lying on the table on Shaw's right. 'What's that?' she enquired, 'your new play?' Shaw nodded. 'Just a bit of nonsense I've written for Robert Loraine for his next tour.' Mrs. Pat glared. 'You promised your next play would be for *me!* Your promises are like pie-crusts, Mr. Shaw, and sorry ones at that.' Shaw nodded, smiling. 'And so it will,' he said, 'I'll write something really good for you. This is only a pot-boiler, you wouldn't like this.' Mrs. Pat picked up the manuscript and examined it. All seemed to be going to plan. 'I was going to read it to D.D.,' said Shaw carelessly, 'but I won't bother, you wouldn't be interested.' But now Mrs. Pat was very interested. 'I'd like to hear a bit of it,' she said, purring with malicious delight at the prospect of playing her favourite indoor game—humiliating authors who had written plays and wished to read them aloud in her presence; old or young, novices or veterans, it didn't matter because she was a past-mistress at the art of dealing with presumption. . . .

'*Pygmalion*, a romance in five acts. Act One, the portico of St Paul's Church, Covent Garden. It is raining, cab whistles are blowing frantically in all directions. . . .' It was two months since he and Mrs. Pat had last met; she had evidently forgotten their conversation for she had no inkling at this point that this was the play which Shaw had promised to write for her. For a time she listened with a slightly bored air, and when Shaw came to Eliza's first cry, 'Aa-ow-ooh,' she saw her chance and took it. 'Oh please, Mr. Shaw,' she drawled with a pained expression on her face, 'not that unpleasant noise; it's not nice.'

MRS. PAT'S REVELATION

For once, the game didn't work. After twenty years of working in the professional theatre, Shaw was well accustomed to leading actresses and their nonsense, and it took more than Mrs. Pat to disconcert him. He ignored her and continued the reading. Presently he repeated the noise much louder, '*Aaaaah-ow-oooh!!*' Mrs. Pat still had no suspicion that this was to be *her* part and that these two dreadful sounds would one day emerge from *her* throat. 'No, no, no, Mr. Shaw,' she protested, a little more firmly this time. 'You really must not make that horrible sound again. It's vulgar!' But a terrible suspicion was beginning to form in her mind . . . could this be? . . . was it? . . . did he *seriously?* . . . *was* it possible . . . ? Shaw continued to ignore her, but when he repeated it worse than ever before, '*Aaaaaaaah-ow-ohh!!!*' trumpeting it at the top of his voice for all Westminster to hear, then suspicion ripened to a certainty. 'You beast,' she stormed, rising from the chaise-longue and confronting him, 'you wrote this play for *me!* I can actually hear you imitating my voice in every line of it!' Of course she was quite right; Shaw was a devastatingly accurate mimic and he was determined that Mrs. Pat should guess the truth without being prompted. They all laughed heartily, Mrs. Pat returned to her chaise-longue and Shaw continued the reading in silence.

She listened intently, nodding and smiling as the comedy developed in ways which appealed to her, and breaking into open laughter during the tea-party scene. Her taste in drama was not infallible but she could recognize quality when she saw it, and Eliza was a superb part . . . but a flower-girl? For *her?* Reassurance came at the end of the play. She was required to speak cockney and to be unwashed only in two acts, and for the remaining three she could be as clean, well-dressed and as ladylike as she pleased. At the end of the reading she had made up her mind to do it, and when Shaw had finished she knew how to rise to the occasion. 'I am deeply flattered, Mr. Shaw,' she intoned in that darkly thrilling voice which had enslaved two continents; and, as befits a famous actress being gracious to a distinguished author, she thanked him for the privilege he had extended to her in reading his beautiful play and offering her the leading part. She returned to the theatre for the evening performance leaving Shaw and Mrs. Lyttleton to congratulate themselves on what had been, they hoped, a very satisfactory afternoon's work.

SHAW'S INFATUATION

Reassurance arrived speedily next day. Mrs. Pat sent Shaw a charmingly business-like letter of appreciation in which she thanked him for reading the play and wondered if, in playing his pretty slut, she might please him. She asked about dates and theatres and actors and invited Shaw to call and see her to discuss what she laughingly described as business. He did not need a second invitation. All unsuspecting, he called at 33 Kensington Square, fully intending to drive a bargain as hard as nails, but things turned out a little differently. Mrs. Pat had decided to enslave him and she succeeded in doing precisely that. She brought into play all her formidable arsenal of charm, flattery, wit and femininity and succeeded in making him fall hopelessly in love in a record time of thirty seconds. Shaw made no resistance; he fell in love, head over ears, and dreamed and dreamed, and walked on air all that day and all the next as if he were once more an adolescent boy. The sirens sang a very sweet song on that hot summer's day, June 28th, 1912. 'I could think of nothing,' he wrote in a rapturous letter to Ellen Terry, 'except a thousand scenes in which she was the heroine and I the hero.' For a married man of fifty-six this was hardly fitting conduct—had he not already enjoyed a long series of love affairs with beautiful and successful women? But this was different: history has recorded few infatuations so ridiculous—or so delicious.

Pygmalion's Opening Night

Stanley Weintraub

Stanley Weintraub recounts *Pygmalion*'s opening night and its aftermath. The play, first produced with the world poised to enter World War I, was notable for its battles between the playwright, Shaw, and his two renowned actors, Mrs. Patrick Campbell and Sir Herbert Beerbohm Tree. But Tree's wretched acting and Mrs. Campbell's attempt to play an eighteen-year-old girl despite being a forty-nine-year-old grandmother all took a backseat to the uttering of one single word: *bloody*. The word was, at the time, a highly offensive expletive, and seemingly no one who watched the play could refrain from voicing an opinion on whether it should be retained in future performances. Stanley Weintraub has taught at Penn State University. He is the author and editor of more than twenty books. In addition to his numerous books on Shaw, he has written biographies on many important nineteenth- and twentieth-century English figures, including Benjamin Disraeli, Queen Victoria, Aubrey Beardsley, and King Edward VII.

His Majesty's Theatre, just above the great intersection where the Haymarket empties into broad, teeming Pall Mall, had reigned by 1914 as London's leading playhouse for seventeen years. Built by actor-manager Herbert Beerbohm Tree out of prudent borrowings from the Prince of Wales's wealthiest financier-friends and the five-figure profits from his immensely successful dramatization of Trilby, it had been at first, in the aged Victoria's honor, Her Majesty's, a palatial structure of red granite and indeterminate limestone which looked as if it had been designed for Louis XV. When it opened in 1897, even the most abrasive dramatic critic in

Excerpted from *Journey to Heartbreak: The Crucible Years of Bernard Shaw, 1914–1918*, by Stanley Weintraub (New York: Weybright & Talley, 1976). Copyright © 1971 by Stanley Weintraub. Reprinted by permission of the author.

London, who signed himself "G.B.S.," [George Bernard Shaw himself] had been impressed. "You feel," he wrote, "that you are in a place where high scenes are to be enacted and dignified things to be done." In the larger of the two commodious rooms in the dome of His Majesty's which had been fashioned into a town residence, Tree gave elaborate after-theatre supper parties, especially after the first night of a play, often hosting them without changing from the costume in which he—inevitably, at his own production—had starred.

OPENING-NIGHT OPTIMISM

Scheduled for opening at His Majesty's on April 11, 1914, was the newest play by the writer who still sometimes signed himself "G.B.S.," and by dint of assiduous self-advertisement and the most literate comedies since Shakespeare's day, had become the best known personality in England. His wife, Charlotte, abroad on a holiday, Shaw left their flat on the upper level of a once stately Georgian house at No. 10 Adelphi Terrace for the twenty-minute walk, alone, to the theatre, up the Strand and around Trafalgar Square, crowded with Saturday sightseers and loungers, into Pall Mall. It was perfect spring weather for walking; the word "halcyon," in fact, seems almost to have been invented to describe the English spring of 1914. Almost everything seemed good, and what did not as yet seem good appeared certain to get better. Science and education seemed to offer the utopian promise that not only was the world capable of infinite improvement, but so were its inhabitants, especially those so fortunate as to live in England. Although this was more illusion than reality, nowhere would that optimism be better symbolized than onstage at His Majesty's. The play, already a box office success in Berlin and Vienna, was a twentieth-century story of a young Cockney guttersnipe who, through a sturdy will and the instruction of a professor of speech, is able to pass for a duchess at a fashionable garden party.

Outside the theatre Bernard Shaw preached the gospel to which he gave life onstage—the need to will one's self-improvement, to redistribute the world's wealth and equalize human opportunity, the abolition of class privilege, and the brotherhood of man. There was little outward reason to expect anything else to happen, in God's good time, and newspapers being hawked on the corners of streets that fed into Trafalgar Square were already giving more attention to

Shaw's play than they were to uneasy stirrings from the Continent, foreshadowings of events that would turn Trafalgar Square, before the end of summer, into a vast, tasteless recruiting platform for the Army. Rumblings of approaching European war were dismissed in most capitals as bluster. The English government believed that the glaring horror of the possibility would in itself be a deterrent—that the war could be so catastrophic to all sides was so obvious that all the Great Powers would shrink from it. The German government believed that the English government believed it.

SHAW VERSUS HIS ACTORS

Backstage at His Majesty's, a war of a different kind had been in progress almost up to the parting of the first curtain. The lack of harmony between the leading actors and the playwright had been in flagrant contradiction to Shaw's past working relationships with his casts, as well as to the comedy's optimistic themes, although in part the stormy mentor-pupil relationship in the play produced onstage sparks akin to those Shaw's direction of the leading lady had been causing in rehearsal. Mrs. Stella Patrick Campbell, in her forty-ninth year and a grandmother, had been the tempestuous beauty of the London theatre since her Mrs. Tanqueray [in Arthur Wing Pinero's play *The Second Mrs. Tanqueray*] more than twenty years earlier, and only a few months before she had encouraged, then spurned, Shaw's most ardent extra-marital advances since his marriage, at forty-two, in 1898. Now, although as unresponsive to Shaw's coaching as she had been to his courting, somehow in performance she had to succeed in shedding her years as the eighteen-year-old Eliza Doolittle. The *Daily Express* was thoroughly ungentlemanly about it on the morning of the opening. "Where is youth these days?" it inquired. "Far from being at the helm it is lucky to be allowed to scrub the decks. A new play is to be performed tonight at His Majesty's. The combined ages of its author, its leading lady and its manager is 166. Sir Herbert is 60, Mr. Shaw is 57 and Mrs. Patrick Campbell, who plays a flower-girl of 18, is 49."

Sir Herbert Beerbohm Tree, the play's Professor Higgins and last of the great Victorian actor-managers, was idiosyncratic, unmethodical, and fawned upon by a claque of satellites who praised, and meddled in, everything he did. Shaw, who produced his own plays, tried to direct the pair of balky prima donnas in how to play *his* roles, but the outcome was unlike anything in his experience. Tree's problem, Shaw said afterwards, was that "he had to impersonate a sort of man he had never met and of whom he had no conception. He tried hard . . . and when he resigned himself to his unnatural task, he set to work to make this disagreeable and incredible person sympathetic in the character of a lover, for which I had left so little room that he was quite baffled. . . ." In the circumstances even the irrepressible Shavian wit found difficulty in emerging, but when Henry Higgins waxed too sentimental over Eliza, Shaw pleaded, "I say, Tree, must you be so treacly?" Tree was not amused, although the remark convulsed everyone else in the theatre, including Henry Dana, Tree's manager, who told him, "You know, Guv'nor, if you put a cat, a dog and a monkey into a sack together, what can you expect but ructions?"

Stella Campbell, certainly the cat of Dana's fable, found Eliza's inelegant diction impossible, but Shaw persisted, once telling her sharply when she tried to conceal her inadequacies in enunciation with irrelevant stage business, "Good God! You are forty years too old for Eliza; sit still and it is not so noticeable." He wrote his comments for specific players on separate sheets, to be distributed after rehearsals, and Mrs. Campbell, with lavatory wit, on one occasion accepted hers with "Thank you, Mr. Shaw, I can always find a good use for a piece of paper!" But when Shaw interrupted a speech to plead that she coarsen her refined stage manner, she refused to continue rehearsals until Shaw left the theatre, and sent word that he was to communicate further instructions only through Stanley Bell, the assistant stage manager. Twice Shaw gathered up his papers and left on his own, once when Mrs. Campbell so badly mangled the accents Shaw had taught her that he abandoned his usual rehearsal location in the center of the dress circle in such haste that he forgot his notes. Returning for them, he heard his Eliza still declaiming her maimed lines and shouted down to her, "Accursed woman, can't you wait till I am out of earshot!"

THE PLAY AS WAR

When out of range, Shaw managed to direct the pair through detailed letters. The immense and caustic pre-opening letter to Tree, Shaw told Mrs. Campbell, "will pull him together if it does not kill him." It did neither. Tree reflected in his note-book instead, "I will not go so far as to say that all people who write letters of more than eight pages are mad, but it is a curious fact that all madmen write letters of more than eight pages." Shaw's last instructions to his Eliza had been entitled "FINAL ORDERS," and in them the playwright re-turned to a favorite source of metaphor—war. Much would depend, he wrote, "on whether you are inspired at the last moment. You are not, like me, a great general. You leave everything to chance, whereas Napoleon and Caesar left nothing to chance except the last inch that is in the hands of destiny. I could have planned the past so that nine tenths of it would have gone mechanically even if your genius had de-serted you, leaving only one tenth to the Gods. Even as it is, I have forced half the battle on you. . . ." Stella responded with a conciliatory note: "I'll obey orders faithfully." She did, and the play was a sensation. Although Shaw's name had long been a household word, after twenty years of playwrit-ing it was his first substantial West End success.

In spite of his rehearsal tribulations, he had assumed the success of the production. *Pygmalion* possessed the leading actress and leading actor-manager in London in starring roles at the most fashionable theatre in London. Further, as he confidently told a reporter from the *Observer*, "It has al-ready been translated into German and Swedish and Polish and Hungarian and it has been performed with monotonous and unbroken success in Germany, Vienna, Stockholm, Prague, Warsaw, Budapest, and the German section of New York." But he ironically confessed his misgivings. "There must be something radically wrong with it if it pleases everybody, but at the moment I cannot find what it is."

ELIZA'S DIRTY WORD

For the public the evening of April 11, 1914, was most mem-orable for Eliza's "Not bloody likely!" The first-night audi-ence gasped with shock, then laughed with such abandon that it threatened the continuity of the play while assuring its success. As the performance continued, Shaw was torn be-tween delight at Mrs. Campbell's ravishment of her audi-ence and rage at Sir Herbert's carefree misunderstanding of his role. To Shaw the conclusion of the play was the most re-lentless travesty of his dramatic intentions he had ever wit-nessed, although the stallholders, unaware of those intentions, left the house in a happy glow. The last Shaw saw of the performance as he hurried out of the theatre before the curtain was "Higgins shoving his mother rudely out of the way and wooing Eliza . . . like a bereaved Romeo." It was exactly what he had painstakingly coached Tree not to do, for G.B.S. felt that only to those incapable of rising above sentimentality did the relationship between Shaw's Galatea [the statue on which the original myth is based] and his Pygmalion appear to have the makings of a marriage. Furious, he refused supper, visits backstage, the privilege of kissing the leading lady, and interviews with the press. Instead he went home alone and soothed his anger by reading Shakespeare for an hour in bed before going to sleep.

The next morning Shaw had settled down sufficiently to invite Stella and her new husband (she had married George Cornwallis-West the week before) to Ayot St. Lawrence for Sunday lunch and tea. Shaw motored up ahead, and they came with Beppo, West's huge black retriever, who distinguished himself by removing people's hats on command and playing hide and seek. Then there were the Sunday papers to discuss, one of which reported some booing when the curtain fell, probably leveled by the righteous at the author whose sanguinary word [bloody] had created such a sensation. Stella brightly suggested that it was directed at Tree by Shavians in the audience infuriated by his acting.

DEFENDING THE DIRTY WORD

While he remained amused by the furor over his six-letter word, Shaw also remained furious about Tree's travesty of the last scene, written to turn romance upside down: Cinderella and the Fairy Prince were supposed to conclude ironically on a note of mutual respect—and dislike—for one another, however much the audience hoped for matrimony. The scene as played caused the *Illustrated London News* to congratulate G.B.S. on his "happy ending, which, when you think of it, you will discover Bernard Shaw is hardly less addicted to than the most confirmed of stage sentimentalists." The bundle of press clippings Shaw sent Charlotte several days after the opening indicated general approval of the play; still, Shaw found it curious that Eliza's expletive remained, even more than the news pages, the chief interest of the press and the public, and popular indignation kept the theatre box office busy. The London newspapers, with two exceptions, found themselves unable to put the terrible word into type, using instead suggestive letters and asterisks. The *Evening Standard* reproached Shaw for an unpardonable breach of good manners, while the *Morning Post* worried that other playwrights, following Shaw's example, would begin sprinkling their works with the lurid language of the street corner. (The *Sketch*, unable to wait for the opening, had published a Saturday editorial begging Shaw to withdraw the naughty word or at least substitute the word "ruddy," and Tree had sent for the author that afternoon to show him a copy and indicate his concern.) "Greatly daring, Mr. Shaw," the *Times* chided on Monday, "you will be able to boast that you are the first modern dramatist to use this word on the stage; but really, was it worth while? There is a whole range of forbidden words in the English language. A little more of your courage, and we suppose they will be heard too; and then good-bye to the delights of really intimate conversation."

A few days later a dispatch indicated that Shaw had removed some of the offense before it became necessary to answer irate bishops in the letters columns of the *Times.* The Cockney guttersnipe, it was said, continued to use the unprintable word, but it was no longer repeated by a young society girl [Clara Eynsford Hill] parroting it because she thought it the latest thing in the slang talk of the smart set. The announcement was premature, but Shaw did ready himself for the bishops before the play had completed its first week by explaining sweetly in an interview in the *Daily News,* "As I happen to find the word detestable when used by a smart, or would-be smart, lady as piece of smartness, and as it was evident that without a strong antidote Mrs. Campbell's irresistible utterance of it would set all smart London bloodying all through the season, I carefully made another lady follow up Mrs. Campbell by repeating that word as a fashionable affectation, with an effect which will, I hope, effectually prevent any occurrence of that folly in real life." Tree tried a different gambit, defending "bloody" to reporters as neither blasphemous nor indecent and hallowed in literary usage from the revered Shakespeare to the moderns. He told reporters the week after the opening,

> Mrs. Patrick Campbell uttered the Word at today's matinee, and nobody was shocked. The only thing which has made the press criticisms so vehement is the flatness of the political sit-

uation. The Word was passed by the Lord Chamberlain and there my responsibility ends. There is nothing blasphemous or obscene in the Word. It may be found in the works of Rudyard Kipling. It may not be good taste for ladies of gentility to wear gaudy feathers in their hat, but they are not obliged to follow Eliza's taste and example either in this or in the use of the Word. Besides I would like to state that a word which is generally applied to Queen Mary Tudor [known as Bloody Mary] should not be censored in a flower-girl.

Unsatisfied, hack playwright Sydney Grundy later in the *Daily Mail* offered the opinion that although there was no harm in Shaw's "incarnadine adverb" when informed by genius, "on his pen it is poison."

The *Daily Express* had shrewdly invited an authentic flower girl to the opening for the purpose of an exclusive interview with her afterward. She was another Eliza—Eliza Keefe of Tottenham Court Road—but apparently better reared than Shaw's Eliza Doolittle, for Mrs. Keefe also objected to the language. "There was one word in particular," she told the *Express,* "which Mrs. Patricia Campbell said when she was supposed to be a lady. The editor says I must not repeat it, but it begins with a B and ends with a Y. *Well!!!* No self-respecting flower girl would say such a word, when she was on her best behaviour, specially when she was supposed to be educated and speaking in a drawing-room."

Letters to the editor on the subject entertained readers of the London dailies for weeks afterward, one in the *Morning Post* summing up how middle-class Englishmen felt, although it was itself very likely tongue-in-cheek and worthy of G.B.S. himself. "The other day," it went, "I was driving down the Haymarket and my taxi happened to collide with another in front. 'Take care, you bloody fool!' shouted my driver. I was about to speak to him most severely when I looked up and there I saw His Majesty's Theatre right in front of me. What Bernard Shaw writes you can hardly blame a cabman for saying."

Triviality manifested itself inside the theatre as well. Tree complained that the play was too long and Mrs. Campbell's costume changes overly prolonged. Mrs. Campbell objected that Tree took thirty-second pauses between each word, and five minutes between each bite of the apple he munched in the fourth act. Still, Tree, happy with a hit grossing more than £2000 a week, suggested hopefully to Shaw that the success had established modern drama at His Majesty's, but rather than the smiles and positive assurances he expected, Tree received curt advice to stop playing for laughs and to never again play Higgins once the current run ended. Fiscally, however, all was optimism. Shaw received £237.9.4 in royalties for the first seven performances, and the play looked as if it could run for years.

CHAPTER 2

Characters

READINGS ON
PYGMALION

Henry Higgins Is Not a Gentleman

J.L. Wisenthal

Henry Higgins may be a scholar, but he is no gentleman, according to J.L. Wisenthal. Higgins's role, like that of the sculptor Pygmalion in the myth, is that of the artist, and he treats Eliza as his creation—a thing—but not as a human being. In his conduct, Higgins is neither a gentleman nor even a man. At times he more resembles a little boy playing with a doll. In his callousness and boorishness, Higgins is contrasted with the play's true gentleman, Colonel Pickering. Despite Pickering's influence on Eliza's manners and self-image, it is Higgins who transforms her. The final scenes are a battle in which Eliza and Higgins vie for superiority, but neither character emerges victorious. Both Eliza's warmth and Higgins's cold professionalism are seen as positive attributes. J.L. Wisenthal has taught at the University of British Columbia. He has written extensively on George Bernard Shaw.

The first point to be grasped about Henry Higgins in *Pygmalion* is that he is, like Dubedat [in Shaw's play *The Doctor's Dilemma*], an artist—as the title of the play implies. He makes a graceless flower girl into a graceful lady, as the sculptor Pygmalion created a beautiful statue out of shapeless stone. Higgins does this by teaching her how to speak correctly and beautifully; phonetics is to be regarded in this play as an artistic as well as scientific pursuit, and elegant speech is to be seen as a valuable accomplishment. Eliza as a lady in Act IV is perhaps less happy than she was as a flower girl—people who are transformed into a higher state usually are not happy in Shaw's plays—but she is superior. (This is perhaps clearer on the stage, where one actually hears the improvement in speech and sees the corresponding improvement in appearance.) The importance and value of the training that Higgins gives to Eliza is stated explicitly in the play in his reply to his mother's charge that he and Pickering are a pair of babies playing with their live doll: "Playing!" he exclaims, "The hardest job I ever tackled: make no mistake about that, mother. But you have no idea how frightfully interesting it is to take a human being and change her into a quite different human being by creating a new speech for her. It's filling up the deepest gulf that separates class from class and soul from soul." Similarly, Shaw in the Preface stresses the crucial role which the phonetician ought to play in society. "The reformer we need most today," he writes, "is an energetic phonetic enthusiast: that is why I have made such a one the hero of a popular play." And later: "If the play makes the public aware that there are such people as phoneticians, and that they are among the most important people in England at present, it will serve its turn."

HENRY'S BEHAVIOR TOWARD ELIZA

Shaw's Pygmalion regards other people not in human terms, but as so much stone to be used for his higher purposes. Therefore he simply cannot understand the concern expressed by Mrs. Pearce and his mother over Eliza's personal future. Mrs. Pearce, on the other hand, understands his lack of concern very well: "Of course I know you dont mean her any harm," she says to him; "but when you get what you call interested in people's accents, you never think or care what may happen to them or you." His behavior to Eliza all through the play is never unkind, but it is always unfeeling. He never tries to hurt her feelings; it is just that he cannot conceive of her (or anyone else) as having any feelings to be hurt.

> PICKERING [*in good-humored remonstrance*] Does it occur to you, Higgins, that the girl has some feelings?
>
> HIGGINS [*looking critically at her*] Oh no, I dont think so. Not any feelings that we need bother about. [*Cheerily*] Have you, Eliza?
>
> LIZA I got my feelings same as anyone else.
>
> HIGGINS [*to Pickering, reflectively*] You see the difficulty?
>
> PICKERING Eh? What difficulty?
>
> HIGGINS To get her to talk grammar. The mere pronunciation is easy enough.

To Higgins, Eliza is merely a thing to be taught (in Acts II and III); then a thing which has been taught (in Act IV); and finally a thing which it would be agreeable and useful to have around the house (in Act V). A human being is not an end in himself with an individual personality that ought to be respected, but the raw material out of which something higher can be made. In Act II Higgins justifies the proposed experiment with Eliza on the ground that "the girl doesnt belong to anybody—is no use to anybody but me," and when in Act V Eliza tells him that Freddy loves her and would make her happy, he replies, "Can he make anything of you? Thats the point."

For Eliza this is not the point at all; she wants a husband who will love and respect her as she is, not one who will make something of her. The fact that Higgins puts forward this particular objection to Freddy reflects his lack of understanding of Eliza. In this lack of human understanding Higgins is like [Jack] Tanner [in Shaw's *Man and Superman*]: he is a master only in his own higher intellectual pursuit, while in dealing with other people (especially women) he is frequently a blunderer. All through the final act Higgins reveals how little he has learned about Eliza during his months of close association with her. When she finally demonstrates that she has become independent of him, he still thinks that she will return to Wimpole Street as a companion: "Now youre a tower of strength: a consort battleship," he says to her. "You and I and Pickering will be three old bachelors together instead of only two men and a silly girl." It would be difficult to imagine terms more ludicrously inappropriate to Eliza, or less likely to appeal to her, than "consort battle ship" and "old bachelor."

GENTLEMAN AND *LADY* AS KEY WORDS

The key words in *Pygmalion* are gentleman and lady: they are used over and over again, with different meanings. In the first act, for example, the Bystander says of Higgins, "E's a genleman: look at his be-oots," while Eliza says of him, "He's no gentleman, he aint, to interfere with a poor girl." In Act II she says to him, "Well, if you was a gentleman, you might ask me to sit down, I think," and she objects to being called a baggage when she has "offered to pay like any lady" for Higgins to enable her to become a "lady in a flower shop." Later she tells Higgins that she wouldn't have eaten his chocolate, "only I'm too ladylike to take it out of my mouth." In Act V the entrance of the newly enriched, formally attired Doolittle is preceded by this dialogue:

> THE PARLORMAID Mr. Henry: a gentleman wants to see you very particular. He's been sent on from Wimpole Street.
>
> HIGGINS . . . Who is it?
>
> THE PARLORMAID A Mr. Doolittle, sir.
>
> PICKERING Doolittle! Do you mean the dustman?
>
> THE PARLORMAID Dustman! Oh no, sir: a gentleman.

Doolittle is identified as a gentleman by his dress, as Higgins was at the start of the play. All of these references (and others) to ladies and gentlemen provide a background to Eliza's well-known speeches to Pickering in Act V about what constitutes ladies and gentlemen: "It was from you that I learnt really nice manners; and that is what makes one a lady, isnt it? You see it was so very difficult for me with the example of Professor Higgins always before me. I was brought up to be just like him, unable to control myself, and using bad language on the slightest provocation. And I should never have known that ladies and gentlemen didnt behave like that if you hadnt been there . . . You see, really and truly, apart from the things anyone can pick up (the dressing and the proper way of speaking, and so on), the difference between a lady and a flower girl is not how she behaves, but how she's treated. I shall always be a flower girl to Professor Higgins, because he always treats me as a flower girl, and always will; but I know I can be a lady to you, because you always treat me as a lady, and always will." Ladies and gentlemen, according to Eliza, are people with "really nice manners" (which include proper speech) and the self-respect that comes from being treated respectfully by others.

HIGGINS VERSUS PICKERING

In the final act Eliza wishes to humiliate Higgins, and therefore she dismisses his role in her education as trivial and says that it was Pickering who really taught her to be a lady. This is unfair to Higgins, without whom she would still be a flower girl. It is true that Pickering has the good manners that Higgins so conspicuously lacks, and it is also true that he was necessary (although not sufficient) for her transformation.

But it was Higgins who conceived the bold idea of transforming Eliza in the first place, and it was his professional skill and perseverance which enabled her to learn to speak—a vital accomplishment for her which she treats too lightly in Act V. Higgins and Pickering are, like Dubedat and Blenkinsop in *The Doctor's Dilemma*, complementary characters, each of them possessing the opposite of the other's qualities and defects. Whereas Dubedat and Blenkinsop force us to consider the relative value of creative genius and moral virtue, Higgins and Pickering force us to consider the relative value of creative genius and good manners. Pickering's manners are as good as Higgins' are bad: Pickering is the perfect gentleman. But Higgins, though no more a real gentleman than Doolittle the dustman is, possesses qualities of a very different kind, which Pickering lacks: like Dubedat, he is the true professional and (as I have noted) artist. The difference between the two characters is brought out in the printed version of the play in the first act, where Pickering is designated "the Gentleman" and Higgins "the Note Taker" (and it is significant in this act that Higgins, who treats Eliza without any consideration, is nevertheless the one who gives her the "large" sum of money). At the beginning of Act II Higgins' professional nature is emphasized by contrast with Pickering; the act begins as Higgins' demonstration of his art ends.

> HIGGINS *[as he shuts the last drawer]* Well, I think thats the whole show.
>
> PICKERING It's really amazing. I havnt taken half of it in, you know.
>
> HIGGINS Would you like to go over any of it again?
>
> PICKERING . . . No, thank you: not now. I'm quite done up for this morning.
>
> HIGGINS . . . Tired of listening to sounds?
>
> PICKERING Yes. It's a fearful strain. I rather fancied myself because I can pronounce twenty-four distinct vowel sounds; but your hundred and thirty beat me. I cant hear a bit of difference between most of them.

It is this professional quality of Higgins to which Eliza principally owes her transformation. We can be certain that Pickering by himself would not have undertaken the experiment, and, as he tells Eliza in Act V, "He [Higgins] taught you to speak; and I couldnt have done that, you know." To this she replies merely, "Of course: that is his profession." For her the only significant acts are those which are done from human, personal motives; she cannot see anything noble or praiseworthy in what a man does as his work. (She tells Higgins that she does not want Freddy to have to work when he is her husband.) We, however, are in a position to see the value in both Pickering's human gentlemanliness and Higgins' zeal and ability, and there is no easy choice to be made between them.

Although Higgins and Pickering are deliberately contrasted characters whose qualities we are to judge in relation to each other, the two of them do not come into conflict at any point in the play; the conflict is between Higgins and Eliza, and it is out of this relationship that the play grows. Eliza is of course a much more complex character than Pickering: whereas the description *"an elderly gentleman of the amiable military type"* leaves little more to be said about him, she cannot be described so easily. For *Pygmalion* is concerned not simply with ladies and gentlemen, but with

COLONEL PICKERING AS A FOIL FOR HENRY HIGGINS

In Pickering, Shaw creates a character whose good manners stand in stark contrast to Henry Higgins's boorishness.

Doolittle is the most obviously 'comic' character in *Pygmalion,* but it would be a mistake to assume that all the play's laughter is associated with him. A great deal of our amusement is caused by Higgins and his outbursts. When he says of Eliza in Act Two 'She's so deliciously low—so horribly dirty—' we laugh almost in spite of ourselves because of his outspokenness, and it is his single-mindedness that amuses us when he instructs Mrs. Pearce to clean Eliza with Monkey Brand, burn all her clothes and wrap her up in brown paper until new ones arrive from the shop. His obsession with his profession causes him to act unconventionally at all times, sometimes very rudely. It is interesting to note how Shaw makes the best comic use of this fact. Higgins on his own would not be very funny, so Shaw has to provide characters who act as the respectable norm beside which he can be judged. Mrs. Pearce with her common sense is one of these characters, but it is necessary for the play's success for there to be another man to contrast with Higgins.

Colonel Pickering is that man and his part in the play is vital. Just as Sherlock Holmes had Doctor Watson in whom to confide his theories, thereby allowing the reader to under-the relationship between this type and women and men (a higher type) and girls and boys (a lower type); and Eliza passes through all three of these stages. She begins in Acts I and II as a flower *girl*; in Acts III and IV she is a lady; and by the end of the play she has become a woman. We have here an ingenious version of the Pygmalion myth: Pygmalion/ Higgins makes the stone/girl into a statue/lady, which Venus/ the Life Force causes to come alive as a woman.

STATUE INTO WOMAN

The interesting part of this development, both in the original myth and in Shaw's handling of it, is the transformation of the statue into a woman. A valuable commentary on this process in *Pygmalion* is provided by a letter that Shaw wrote to the actress Florence Farr in 1891—twenty-one years before he wrote the play—while he was giving her elocution and voice lessons: "Prithee persevere with the speaking: I found with unspeakable delight last time that you were be-

---

stand the processes of the great detective's mind, so Pickering is the audience's representative in the play. Although we gather that he is an expert on Sanskrit, he merely gives the impression of being amiable and slightly stupid. His caution and good manners contrast with Higgins's volatile qualities, and help us to understand the Professor better. He admires Higgins's abilities and in the tea-party scene at Mrs. Higgins's home is quite carried away with excitement about the project of passing Eliza off as a lady, so that we have the comic spectacle of the two men shouting simultaneously about the way Eliza's education is going. Occasionally Shaw allows Pickering to make some remark that is funny in a theatrical way without being witty in itself, as in the following exchange:

> MRS. HIGGINS: Colonel Pickering: dont you realise that when Eliza walked into Wimpole Street, something walked in with her?

> PICKERING: Her father did. But Henry soon got rid of him.

In general, however, he is the calm character who acts as a foil to Higgins and perhaps causes us to sympathise with him more than we should do otherwise; if a decent, humane man like Pickering finds Higgins amiable, perhaps we, the audience, can overlook some of his selfishness and conceit and find him likeable as well as witty.

G.E. Brown, *George Bernard Shaw.* New York: Arco, 1971.

ginning to do it quite beautifully. There is much more to be done, of course, much ill usage in store for you, but success is now certain. You have reached the stage of the Idiotically Beautiful. There remain the stages of the Intelligently Beautiful & finally of the Powerfully Beautiful; & until you have attained the last you will never be able to compel me to recognize the substance of that soul of which I was shown a brief image by Nature for her own purposes." This letter is indeed remarkable as an anticipation of *Pygmalion*—even its final sentence is echoed in Higgins' references to Eliza in Act V as a soul and as a part of humanity "that has come my way and been built into my house." And the progression that Shaw sets out in the letter corresponds exactly to Eliza's development in the last three acts of the play. In Act III, at Mrs. Higgins' At Home, she is Idiotically Beautiful; she is an artificial duchess, a live doll, a statue. The fact that she is now fit for the Eynsford Hills's society implies that many of the middle class never evolve beyond the statue stage, that they never become human. In Act IV she has reached the level of the Intelligently Beautiful; she is a lady not only in her accent and dress, but also in her possession of a new sensitivity, a delicacy of feeling that has hitherto been lacking. With this sensitivity she becomes aware that Higgins has no human feeling for her and regards her as a mere thing, and she therefore determines to be independent of him. This she achieves in a limited way in Act IV, when she reviles him bitterly and leaves Wimpole Street, and in a final, thorough way in Act V, when she repudiates his dominance exultantly, announcing that she will marry Freddy and support him by teaching phonetics as an assistant to Higgins' rival. The exchange that follows this declaration is the climax of the play:

> HIGGINS *[rising in a fury]* What! That impostor! that humbug! that toadying ignoramus! Teach him my methods! my discoveries! You take one step in his direction and I'll wring your neck. *[He lays hands on her]*. Do you hear?
>
> LIZA *[defiantly non-resistant]* Wring away. What do I care? I knew youd strike me some day. *[He lets her go, stamping with rage at having forgotten himself, and recoils so hastily that he stumbles back into his seat on the ottoman]*. Aha! Now I know how to deal with you. What a fool I was not to think of it before! You cant take away the knowledge you gave me. You said I had a finer ear than you. And I can be civil and kind to people, which is more than you can. Aha! *[Purposely dropping her aitches to annoy him]* Thats done you, Enry Iggins, it

az. Now I dont care that *[snapping her fingers]* for your bullying and your big talk. I'll advertize it in the papers that your
duchess is only a flower girl that you taught, and that she'll
teach anybody to be a duchess just the same in six months for
a thousand guineas. Oh, when I think of myself crawling under your feet and being trampled on and called names, when
all the time I had only to lift up my finger to be as good as
you, I could just kick myself.

HIGGINS *[wondering at her]* You damned impudent slut, you!
But it's better than snivelling; better than fetching slippers
and finding spectacles, isnt it? *[Rising]* By George, Eliza, I
said I'd make a woman of you; and I have. I like you like this.

This is the moment at which the sculptor secs with delighted
amazement that his statue has come to life. Eliza is now
Powerfully Beautiful: no longer a flower girl, more than a
mere lady—a woman, who has sufficient vitality and
strength of will to face life with courage and self-reliance.

HIGGINS IS MORE BOY THAN MAN

Where does this leave Higgins? One point to be noted is that
his statement "I said I'd make a woman of you; and I have"
is not quite correct. He said he would make a lady, "a
duchess," of her; it is the Life Force inherent in Eliza herself
that has enabled her to become a woman (although Higgins
has helped by bullying and offending her to the point where
she revolts against him). And if she is a woman, what is he?
According to the concept of "woman" which is implicit in his
speech to her, he is a man; he has already boasted of his own
self-reliance. But in other senses he is not a man. he is inhuman and immature, which is to say that he is a brute
rather than a man and a boy rather than a man. . . . Higgins
is described in the stage direction that introduces him as
"rather like a very impetuous baby," and is treated as such by
his mother, for whom he feels a child's affection; and he
himself says to Pickering in Act II that he has "never been
able to feel really grown-up and tremendous, like other
chaps." Whereas Eliza has become by the end of the play
both a lady and a woman, Higgins is neither a gentleman
nor (in important senses of the term) a man.

NEITHER HIGGINS NOR ELIZA IS VICTORIOUS

This does not mean, however, that Eliza is the outright victor.
She does, it is true, humiliate Higgins in the final act, particularly in the last part. . . . But Higgins, though humiliated by

Eliza, is still superior to her in significant ways. He is the creator of Eliza the lady, and only as a lady could she have become a woman—or so the play implies. He propounds an ideal, by which his own life is governed, which Eliza can neither understand nor live by: the ideal of a cold life of impersonal striving. Eliza, on the other hand, propounds *her* ideal: a warm life of personal friendship and love. During the discussion between Higgins and Eliza in Act V, these two ideals, and the characters who embody them, are beautifully balanced; only at the end does Eliza seem to emerge triumphant—and even then one feels that the issue has not been finally decided. During the discussion, we have the impression that Higgins is utterly vanquished, then Eliza, then Higgins, and so on. With each speech an unexpected other side to the question springs into view. On the day on which *Pygmalion* opened in London, Shaw sent Mrs. Patrick Campbell [the actress who played Eliza in the play's London premiere] a letter headed "FINAL ORDERS," which included the following: "If you have ever said to Stella [Mrs. Patrick Campbell's daughter] in her childhood 'I'll let you see whether you will . . . obey me or not,' and then inverted her infant shape and smacked her until the Square (not to mention the round) rang with her screams, you will . . . know how to speak the line 'I'll let you see whether I'm dependent on you.' There is a certain dragging intensity, also used in Act IV in 'YOU thank God etc,' which is wanted here to re-establish your lead after Higgins' long speech about science and classical music and so on. The author took care to re-establish it by giving Eliza a long and energetic speech in reply to him; but the ignorant slave entrusted with the part thought she knew better than the author, and cut out the speech as useless. Now she has got to do it the other way."

The line "I'll let you see whether I'm dependent on you," which Shaw removed from the play when revising the scene for the film version, occurred shortly after Eliza's reply to Higgins' "science and classical music" speech. What Shaw is saying to Mrs. Patrick Campbell in the letter is that since she has dropped the "long and energetic speech" that he had provided to re-establish Eliza's lead (that is, the one beginning "Oh, you are a cruel tyrant,") she would have to re-establish it by giving special emphasis to the later speech. The phrase "re-establish your lead" neatly sums up Shaw's "tennis" technique in the last scene of *Pygmalion,* and in the debates which provide the climaxes of many of his other plays. . . . Eliza and Higgins keep re-establishing their respective leads, until the play ends with no clear victory for either of them. The play does not take one side or the other; it leaves us valuing both Eliza's warm human qualities and Higgins' cold professional qualities, and it leaves us faced with the dilemma that arises from the incompatibility of these two sets of virtues, perfection of the life and of the work.

Higgins's Anti-Romantic Character

David J. Gordon

Shaw titled *Pygmalion* "A Romance," but David J. Gordon contends that the play works against this characterization. The Cinderella fantasy is irresistible, but everything about the character of Henry Higgins resists a romantic liaison with the transformed flower girl. For Higgins to succeed as a character, he must be harsh as well as attractive. And he cannot marry. Higgins is a man, not unlike Shaw, whose excessive admiration for his mother leads him to resist a woman whom he might otherwise love. The entire plot of *Pygmalion* derives from this anti-romantic notion, as the play's action keeps moving toward romance and then backing off. David J. Gordon has taught at Hunter College and at the City University of New York graduate center. His works include *D.H. Lawrence as a Literary Critic, Literary Art and the Unconscious, Iris Murdoch's Fables of Unselfing,* and *Bernard Shaw and the Comic Sublime,* from which this excerpt is taken.

[*Pygmalion*] is subtitled A Romance, and certainly it generates thoroughly romantic expectations up to a point. Few literary fantasies are as irresistible as this Cinderellan metamorphosis of the cockney flower girl into the supposed princess at an ambassador's party. It is sometimes said that the momentum of this romance plot is so strong that the romantic dénouements perpetrated by Sir Beerbohm Tree and Mrs. Patrick Campbell (to Shaw's disgust) and later by others, including Messrs Lerner and Loewe [in the musical *My Fair Lady*], are justified. But Shaw was nowhere more faithful to his own distinctive sensibility than in those potent structures of disappointment, acts 4 and 5. The Miltonic [re-

ferring to the English poet John Milton] mind of Higgins and
the eloquent humanity of Eliza are opposed in an absolute
stalemate. There can be no compromise between the expectations of acts 1–3 and the disappointment of 4–5, as Shaw
himself managed to prove by trying unsuccessfully to write
a narrative continuation about Eliza's moderately happy future with Freddy, pages described accurately by [critic Mau-
rice] Valency as 'dismally novelistic.' Shaw was, at one and
the same time, romantic and anti-romantic, and this am-
bivalence is especially firm in *Pygmalion*. It is right that Higgins is alone at the end, laughing in denial of his failure to
hold Eliza. And Eliza must be disappointed too, for the man
she cannot help loving is incorrigible. Her whole story—the
fantastic rise and its unexpectedly bitter end—is replayed in
a farcical key by the story of Doolittle, her father.

HIGGINS'S CHARACTER

Shaw knew that, at the peril of sentimentality, Higgins must
be harsh as well as attractive. It is no accident that *Pygmalion* is the most candid of his works on the subject of incest. Higgins's incapacity for sexual love despite his unconscious seductiveness is explicitly traced to his idealisation of
a superior mother. Shaw does not resort here to either of his
two favourite explanations for the prevailing taboo on incest.
One, drily rationalistic, is that early familiarity kills romance. The other comes closer to the truth by being its exact opposite: a mother's love is too much for a child and
overwhelms him. *Pygmalion* is unique among his plays in
encouraging us to make a connection between a character's
early, excessive admiration of a mother and his later resistance to a woman he could otherwise love.

To suggest that Higgins represents Shaw's most direct effort of dramatic self-confrontation is not to say naïvely that
he is a proxy for the author, much less a puppet, for we are
dealing with an imaginative configuration, 'the dancing of
an attitude' in [literary critic] Kenneth Burke's nice phrase,
not with mere personal characteristics. The preface adverts
us to a brilliant, arrogant phonetician named Henry Sweet as
the original for Higgins, a proud and impatient man who did
not suffer fools gladly. . . . The arrogance of Higgins is
mainly expressed as an amiable bullying, aggressive enough
yet peculiarly innocent in its unguarded directness. The
most important device for distancing him is to make his ag-

gressive abruptness look comical by virtue of his lack of self-consciousness. Probably the most effective of a dozen such passages occurs in act 4, after the party:

> LIZA . . . What's to become of me?
>
> HIGGINS [*enlightened, but not at all impressed*] Oh, *thats* whats worrying you, is it? *[He thrusts his hands into his pockets, and walks about in his usual manner, rattling the contents of his pockets, as if condescending to a trivial subject out of pure kindness] I* shouldnt bother about it if I were you. I should imagine you wont have much difficulty in settling yourself somewhere or other, though I hadnt quite realized that you were going away. *[She looks quickly at him: he does not look at her, but examines the dessert stand on the piano and decides that he will eat an apple]* You might marry, you know. *[He bites a large piece out of the apple and munches it noisily]*.

Higgins's speech is a masterly, half-unconscious effort both to attract and repel. The final stage direction caps his character beautifully. Shaw's turn of phrase *('he eats his apple with a dreamy expression of happiness, as it is quite a good one')* so neatly justifies Higgins from his own point of view and condemns him from ours.

HIGGINS AND ELIZA

But though we may laugh at him, Shaw insisted that he must be heroic. One of the play's insights is that intellectual or creative achievement may be significantly related to the continued presence of early idealisations. But heroic need not mean likeable, and indeed usually does not. The mother's exasperation with her son and Pickering who are playing like boys with a live doll and Eliza's anguished slipper-throwing are human protests, forcefully expressed, against the inhumanity of an heroic stance.

The romance of Eliza's rise is given considerable space before the shadows fall. Her naïveté in the early acts is extremely charming, and her father's comparable casuistry [false reasoning] is unusually disarming. But sorrow is drawn *from* the romance. Eliza owes her transformation to a Pygmalion who must, we can see from the first, fail to live quite up to his mythic role at the last. And Doolittle's 'fall' into middle-class morality has, in a sense, been his own doing. We may regret the forlorness, but anti-climax is a central feature of Shaw's sensibility and I can readily understand his impatience with the softened ending. Higgins is so fully and honestly imagined that he really must not be allowed to toss Eliza a kiss or a rose. And bringing Freddy forward as a companion for Eliza has really nothing to do with the story of her romance. Of course, it is reasonable to assume that a young woman, romantically disappointed, will eventually make a new, more prosaic life for herself, but this makes another story.

The strength of *Pygmalion* has much to do with the unresolved tension between the 'higher' consciousness of Higgins and the 'lower' consciousness of Eliza. It is a sexually charged tension that insists on both eternal separateness and eternal reciprocity. Not every viewer or reader finds aesthetic satisfaction in that. But it may help to show how the impasse of acts 4 and 5 is prepared by the romance of the first three acts.

AN ANTI-ROMANTIC PLOT

Each of the early acts gracefully develops a romantic situation and at the curtain gracefully turns it away. We start with a wonderful whirl of contrasting voices—the fretful Eynsford-Hills sending off their Freddy to look for a cab in the rain, the broad cockney whine of the flower girl, the nonchalant

---

THE MODEL FOR HENRY HIGGINS

Shaw modeled his professor of phonetics, Henry Higgins, on the well-known, eccentric English linguist Henry Sweet.

Bernard Shaw entitles his preface to *Pygmalion* "A Professor of Phonetics." The reference is to the distinguished scholar, Henry Sweet. It is evident that Shaw took Sweet as a model for some of the major lineaments of the portrait of the Professor Higgins of the play. It was Sweet who invented the *Broad Romic* system of phonetic notation; it was Sweet who sent postcards in that script and in his shorthand script to his friends; it was Sweet who was able to pronounce distinctly seventy-two vowel sounds. Sweet would often turn his back on a group of speakers and jot down a phonetic record of their conversation; Sweet was engrossed in his studies—as is Professor Higgins—to the exclusion of the social amenities; and Sweet alone, in England, was sufficiently the master of the science of phonetics to have been able to transmute Liza into Miss Doolittle.

Bertrand M. Wainger, "Henry Sweet—Shaw's Pygmalion," *Studies in Philology*, vol. 27, 1930.

echoing of the Notetaker punctuated by the remarks of suspicious bystanders—and gradually rising from the mêlée, as the rain unnoticeably stops, the educated exchange of Pickering and Higgins playing out an irresistibly improbable recognition scene. They joke amiably about what Eliza could be and, with godlike condescension, shower her with coins. She goes off self-importantly but alone in the cab that Freddy finally obtained for his family, who have already left.

The second and third acts are constructed similarly, a movement of building up and dashing romance that is half-concealed by the charm of the humour and the expectation of later fulfilment. In the first part of act 2, Eliza arrives at Wimpole Street with her new wealth to hire Higgins as a teacher, and amid a good deal of bullying and scorn, the romantic wager is made. Enter thereupon a sordid complication, the blackmailing dustman. But he so beguiles the gentlemen and us with his casuistic defence of the undeserving poor that we do not realise, until his charismatic presence fades, that the boy-gentlemen have taken on a 'stiff job' of a less technical and more complexly human kind than they are prepared to acknowledge.

Mrs. Higgins serves much the same deflationary function in the third act that Doolittle does in the second. Higgins and then Pickering enter her drawing room excitedly, arousing our expectation of a transformed Eliza performing successfully before an audience of Eynsford-Hills. We are struck for a moment by the element of truth in Higgins's statement that a change of class is like a change of soul. Then our Galatea [the statue in the original Pygmalion myth] regresses to street talk, charming Freddy and delighting Clara. But Mrs. Higgins soberly and forcefully points out to us that the two 'infinitely stupid male creatures' are toying with a human life. The picture of her at the curtain (scorning men! men!! men!!!) registers one of his strongest judgements against his own kind of inhumanity, drawing its strength from his investment in the image of the judging mother.

With the structure of these acts in mind, we see more clearly that, despite further comic moments (notably the tophatted Doolittle complaining about Ezra D. Wannafeller's Moral Reform Society and Pre-Digested Cheese Trust), the fourth and fifth acts dramatise a sustained impasse. Love is in the air but checked, stifled. The fourth act plays off Higgins's triumphant egotism against Eliza's human anguish.

Baffled, she throws his gift ring into the fireplace, picks it out again and flings it once more on to a dessert stand. The fifth act sustains this mood with the addition of other voices—Mrs. Higgins's, Pickering's, Doolittle's. Mrs. Higgins's role is to explain to the men the full humanity of Eliza. Pickering is now differentiated more clearly from Higgins, as adumbrated by his earlier politeness. Higgins naturally remains incorrigible: 'Get up and come home; and dont be a fool.' 'Very nicely put', replies his mother, 'No woman could resist such an invitation.'

HIGGINS AND DOOLITTLE

He is, in fact, throughout the play, much like the incorrigible Doolittle, both in his chief virtues—utter frankness and freedom from snobbery—and in his chief vice—thinking of Eliza as a thing to manipulate. The difference is that Doolittle blandly resorts to blackmail whereas the heroically minded Higgins wants to make something of her, and scorns Freddy as a suitor because he cannot, in his terms, do so. Higgins is sincere in contrasting his own offer of a life devoted to Science and Literature with marriage to a man who can only offer money, kisses and kicks. But Eliza, though pained by the knowledge that she must give up much of higher value in making a decent, common life for herself, is resolved to do so and to do so with a measure of dignity. A harshly comic mutual rejection stamps the final moment of action. She sweeps out with mock indifference of his need for her; he laughs excessively at the idea of her marrying Freddy.

Shaw makes it clear that heartbreak is inevitable in either the lofty or the common life yet that each is to be respected. He checks his two most characteristic impulses—to transcend and to ridicule—and thus in effect renders judgement on his own vision.

Alfred Doolittle's Role in the Play

Louis Crompton

According to Louis Crompton, Alfred Doolittle's role in *Pygmalion* mirrors that of his daughter. He is brought out of poverty by a twist of fate and is forced to change his lifestyle, his manners, and, beyond this, his morality. But whereas Eliza wishes to rise to the respectable middle class, her father realizes that his low social standing had given him moral immunity: He was able to do whatever he wanted and get away with it; nothing was expected of him. For Shaw, Doolittle's poverty ironically makes his life too easy. Doolittle's move to middle-class morality is a shattering blow to the dustman. As suggested by Doolittle's and his daughter's rise, the central theme of the play is the passion for improving the human race versus the ordinary human desire to live comfortably. Louis Crompton has taught at the University of Nebraska. He has published several books on George Bernard Shaw.

Professor Higgins, Shaw's Prometheus of phonetics, is . . . without manners. Consider the Olympian tirade he visits on Eliza's head while she sits snivelling in Covent Garden:

> A woman who utters such depressing and disgusting sounds has no right to be anywhere—no right to live. Remember that you are a human being with a soul and the divine gift of articulate speech: that your native language is the language of Shakespear and Milton and The Bible; and dont sit there crooning like a bilious pigeon.

Clearly, the man who can vent such splendid wrath upon a street vendor is neither a snob nor a vulgarian, but neither is he a gentleman, and he just as certainly has no more manners than the petulant daughter or the disgruntled flower girl. At home he takes his boots off and wipes his hands on his dressing gown. In creating Higgins, Shaw was assuredly driving at something more than a definition of true gentility.

Before we consider what it is, however, we may pause for a moment to look at the part Eliza's father, Alfred Doolittle, plays in the comedy. Here Shaw turns from the question of social manners to the deeper question of social morality. The farce of the dustman turned moral preacher has always delighted Shaw's audiences. But just as they have rested content with the Cinderella aspect of the main story, so the ironic intention in this second transformation has been missed. One critic has even held that since Doolittle is less happy after coming into his fortune than he was before, Shaw's aim was to demonstrate the "vanities of philanthropy." This is not so much to miss Shaw's point as to turn it completely upside down. What Shaw is saying is that Doolittle after his escape from Lisson Grove is a much better social being, albeit a less comfortable one, than he was before. Critics have simply overlooked the ironic amusement with which Shaw views the dustman's discomfiture, which he regards as pure gain from the point of view of society.

Shaw seems to have been inspired to create the fable of Doolittle's sudden wealth by [English novelist Charles] Dickens' use of a similar story in one of his novels. In *Our Mutual Friend*, Dickens contrasts two poor men, one a Thames-side water rat named "Rogue" Riderhood, and the other an honest garbage collector, Mr. Boffin, who unexpectedly comes into a large inheritance. Each is treated as an all-black or all-white figure in a popular melodrama. Riderhood, whom Dickens describes bluntly as a piece of "moral sewage," remains unrelievedly villainous throughout, while Boffin, a kind of illiterate Pickwick [an eccentric Dickens character], is a paragon of benevolence both before he becomes wealthy and after. Shaw's approach is to roll Dickens' pair of poor men into one, and then to show how the man's behavior is a consequence not of his character, but of his situation.

Alfred Doolittle first appears in Wimpole Street in the hypocritical role of virtuous father, rather after the fashion of Engstrand in [playwright Henrik] Ibsen's *Ghosts*, his intention being to blackmail the two men who have taken up Eliza. When Higgins bullies him out of this scheme, he changes his tack and becomes the ingratiating pimp: "Well, the truth is, Ive taken a sort of fancy to you, Governor; and if you want the girl, I'm not so set on having her back home again but that I might be open to an arrangement." This approach fails too. But Doolittle is nothing if not a resourceful rhetorician. He forthwith throws morality to the winds and argues for consideration, in an eloquent flight of philosophical oratory, as an undeserving poor man done out of his natural right to happiness by the narrow-minded prejudices of middle-class morality. Higgins and Pickering, enchanted, now offer him five pounds, which he accepts after rejecting ten as too likely to entail sobering responsibilities. But alas, the man who shrinks from ten pounds comes into several thousand a year before the play is over and finds his free and easy life at an end. What, then, is the meaning of this fable?

First of all, Doolittle's moral and social attitudes contrast strongly with Eliza's. Eliza yearns above all things to join the respectable lower middle class. Doolittle, finding that his job as garbage collector is too low on the social scale to have any moral standards attached to it, realizes that he already has, in a sense, the prerogatives of a duke, and is loath to rise. He protests that he likes a little "ginger" in his life, "ginger" to his mind being the privilege of beating his female paramours, changing them at will, indulging in periodic drinking bouts, and pursuing life, liberty, and happiness on his own terms. But Shaw, like [English writer Thomas] Carlyle, did not consider personal happiness the end of human existence. Hollow as three-quarters of middle-class morality may be, and damaging to the race on its higher levels, the imposition of minimum standards of decency on Doolittle is clear gain, any standards being better than the impunity he enjoys as a result of his poverty. If we leave his engaging impudence aside, it is a difficult thing to admire a man who wants to sell his daughter, and it is impossible to like a blackmailer. Shaw's aim as a socialist was to abolish the poor as a class on the grounds that such people were dangerous and contemptible. Shaw held it against poverty that it made Doolittle's kind of happiness all too easy. In a Shavian Utopia the Industrial Police would no doubt have bundled Doolittle off to a labor camp with as little compunction as they would a rent-collecting millionaire who took a similar view as to the world's owing him a living. Doolittle's character does not change, but he is as effectively moralized by coming into money as any hooligan athlete who has ever won a world's championship or any hillbilly moonshiner whose land has brought him a fortune in oil royalties. When

Higgins, on the occasion of his marriage, asks if he is an honest man or a rogue, his answer is "A little of both, Henry, like the rest of us." Doolittle is, in short, whatever society wants to make of him.

Conventional farce would have ended with Eliza's fiasco at Mrs. Higgins' at-home, conventional romance with her triumph at the ambassador's reception and a love match between her and Higgins. But Shaw contended that most ordinary plays became interesting just when the curtain fell. What, he wants to know, will be Galatea's relation to her creator after the transformation has taken place? It was one of his favorite theories that people of high culture appear to savages or even to the average man as cold, selfish, and unfeeling simply because of their inaccessibility to the common emotions and their freedom from ordinary affectionateness or jealousy. The development of Eliza's relation to the professor in the last two acts is meant to illustrate this perception.

Higgins is in many ways a paradoxical being. He is at once a tyrannical bully and a charmer, an impish schoolboy and a flamboyant wooer of souls, a scientist with a wildly extravagant imagination and a man so blind to the nature of his own personality that he thinks of himself as timid, modest, and diffident. Like Caesar in [Shaw's play] *Caesar and Cleopatra,* he is part god and part brute; but unlike Caesar, he cannot boast that he has "nothing of man" in him. It is this manliness, which takes the form of obtuseness to the feelings of others, that leads to his first comeuppance. He and Pickering alike have both failed to grasp the fact that Eliza's heroic efforts to improve herself have not been based merely on a desire to rise in the world, and still less on any desire for perfection for its own sake, but are first of all the result of a doglike devotion to two masters who have taken trouble over her. When the men fail to pet and admire her after her triumph, her thwarted feelings turn to rage, and, desperate to provoke an emotional response from Higgins, she needles him so she may enjoy the spectacle of a god in a vulgar human fury.

Yet however much her spitfire vehemence may put us in mind of the street girl, the Eliza of this scene is far from the original Eliza of Covent Garden. There is a new dignity and even calculation in her emotional outburst. She has now mastered more than the pronunciation of the educated classes. When she meets Higgins at his mother's the next morning she is a model of poised reserve, even cuttingly cold in manner. Obviously her old commonness has forsaken her at the very moment that the experiment has ended and she must find her way independently in life. Nevertheless, Eliza's development, marked though it is, is limited in one important respect. She never gets past the stage of judging the world wholly in relation to herself. In this respect she remains a typical petite bourgeoise, who, as Higgins puts it, sees life and personal relations in commercial terms. She has nothing of the impersonality of the world-betterer, nothing of Higgins's scientific passion for reform. Once again, as with Caesar and Cleopatra, it is a case of the superhuman face to face with the all-too-human. Higgins tells Eliza he cares "for life, for humanity," and her objection is that he does not care personally for *her.* On hearing that she is going to marry Freddy, Clara's amiable but brainless brother, Higgins objects—"Can he make anything of you?" He is chagrined at seeing his duchess, so to speak, thrown away. Eliza in her turn finds such a question unintelligible: "I never thought of us making anything of one another; and you never think of anything else. I only want to be natural."

To all but the most inveterate sentimentalist the relation between Eliza and her mentor does not appear to have the makings of a marriage. Higgins lacks not only the personal tenderness Eliza craves but even the tact necessary to avoid hurting her repeatedly. Not that he wants cunning in his treatment of women. He knows, Eliza tells him, "how to twist the heart in a girl." But in the end, Higgins, who has devoted his life "to the regeneration of the human race through the most difficult science in the world," does not need a wife. . . . Higgins explains to Eliza that he has grown accustomed to her face and voice and that he likes them as he likes his furniture, but he makes it brutally clear that he can also get on without them and that he does not really need her. Knowledge of these facts does not endear him to Eliza, who infinitely prefers Freddy's simple-hearted homage. As Shaw tells us in his prose sequel to the play, "Galatea never does quite like Pygmalion: his relation to her is too godlike to be altogether agreeable." Eliza is not yearning after godhead; she likes Freddy Eynsford Hill.

The central theme of *Pygmalion* is the contrast between the Promethean passion for improving the race and the ordinary human desire for the comforts and consolations of the domestic hearth.

Eliza Grows Up in Acts Four and Five

Eric Bentley

Eric Bentley suggests that *Pygmalion* is a problematic play because it seems anticlimatic to many. The last two acts may seem to be merely a discussion of the ramifications of Henry Higgins's experiment. But the play is about more than passing Eliza Doolittle off as a duchess. Higgins has made her into a lady, but that is not Shaw's main concern. Eliza must become a real woman, she must grow into her own independence, and this is Shaw's interest as the play works its way through the last two acts. Eric Bentley is a renowned drama critic, author, and translator whose books include *The Playwright as Thinker*, *What Is Theatre?*, and *Modern Theatre*.

Pygmalion is the story, in five Acts, of Henry Higgins' attempt to make a duchess out of a flower girl. Act I is really a sort of prologue in which the two main characters encounter each other. The action proper starts in Act II when Higgins decides to make the experiment. In Act III the experiment reaches its first stage when Eliza appears in upper-class company behaving like an imperfectly functioning mechanical doll. Readers of [French philosopher and writer Henri] Bergson will understand why this scene gets more laughs than all of the others put together, so that to the groundlings the rest of the play seems a prolonged anti-climax. Has not Shaw blundered? What ought to be the climax seems to have been left out: it is between Acts III and IV that Eliza is finally passed off as a duchess at an ambassador's party. . . . When the curtain goes up on Act IV all is over; Eliza has triumphed. Higgins is satisfied, bored, and wondering what to do next. The comedy is over. But there are two more acts!

THE CONSEQUENCES OF CREATION

Certainly, the big event occurs between the Acts, and the last
two Acts *are* a "discussion" of the consequences.... It is not
so much that the consequences are discussed as that the
consequences are worked out and determined by a conflict
that is expressed in verbal swordplay. There is no pretence
of objectivity. Each character speaks for himself, and speaks,
not as a contributor to a debate, but as one whose life is at
stake. Eliza is talking to free herself. Higgins is talking to
keep his domination over her. The conclusion of conversations of this kind is not the statement of a principle . . . but
the making of a decision. [Norwegian playwright Henrik] Ibsen's Nora slams the door, his Ellida decides to stay at home.
What happens to Eliza? What *can* happen, now that the
flower girl is a duchess, the statue a flesh-and-blood Galatea
[the female statue in the original myth of Pygmalion]?

In the original romance, so lyrically revived by Shaw's
friend [the English writer] William Morris, [the sculptor]
Pygmalion marries Galatea. Might not something of the kind
be possible for Shaw, since Pygmalion is a life-giver, a sym-
bol of vitality, since in Eliza the crime of poverty has been
overcome, the sin of ignorance cancelled? Or might not Higgins and Eliza be the "artist man" and "mother woman" discussed in [Shaw's play] *Man and Superman?* They might—if
Shaw actually went to work so allegorically, so abstractly, so
idealistically. Actually *Pygmalion: a Romance* stands related
to Romance precisely as [Shaw's play] *The Devil's Disciple*
stands to Melodrama or [Shaw's play] *Candida* to Domestic
Drama. It is a serious parody, a translation into the language
of "natural history." The primary inversion is that of Pygmalion's character. The Pygmalion of Romance turns a
statue into a human being. The Pygmalion of "natural history" tries to turn a human being into a statue, tries to make
of Eliza Doolittle a mechanical doll in the role of a duchess.
Or rather he tries to make from one kind of doll—a flower
girl who cannot afford the luxury of being human—another
kind of doll—a duchess to whom manners are an adequate
substitute for morals.

There is a character named Pygmalion in *Back to
Methuselah.* He is a sort of Frankenstein [scientist in the
novel of the same name] or [Russian scientist Ivan] Pavlov.
He thinks that you can put together a man by assembling
mechanical parts. Henry Higgins also thinks he has made a

person—or at least an amenable slave—when he has "assembled" a duchess. But the monster turns against Frankenstein. Forces have been brought into play of which the man-maker knows nothing. And Shaw's Pygmalion has helped into being a creature even more mysterious than a monster: a human being.

If the first stage of Higgins' experiment was reached when Eliza made her *faux pas* before Mrs. Higgins' friends, and the second when she appeared in triumph at the ball, Shaw, who does not believe in endings, sees her through two more stages in the final acts of his play, leaving her still very much in flux at the end. The third stage is rebellion. Eliza's feelings are wounded because, after the reception, Higgins does not treat her kindly, but talks of her as a guinea pig. Eliza has acquired finer feelings.

While some have felt that the play should end with the reception, others have felt that it could end with the suggestion that Eliza has begun to rebel. It seems, indeed, that the creator of the role of Eliza thought this. In her memoirs Mrs. Patrick Campbell [the actress who first played Eliza on stage] wrote:

> The last act of the play did not travel across the footlights with as clear dramatic sequence as the preceding acts—owing entirely to the fault of the author.

THE NECESSARY FIFTH ACT

The sympathetic analyst of the play will more probably agree with Shaw himself who, Mrs. Campbell says, "declared I might be able to play a tune with one finger, but a full orchestral score was Greek to me." The fifth Act of *Pygmalion* is far from superfluous. It is the climax. The arousing of Eliza's resentment in the fourth Act was the birth of a soul. But to be born is not enough. One must also grow up. Growing up is the fourth and last stage of Eliza's evolution. This consummation is reached in the final "discussion" with Higgins—a piece of dialogue that is superb comedy not only because of its wit and content but also because it proceeds from a dramatic situation, perhaps the most dramatic of all dramatic situations: two completely articulate characters engaged in a battle of words on which both their fates depend. It is a Strindbergian [after the Swedish playwright August Strindberg] battle of wills. But not of sex. Higgins will never marry. He wants to remain in the relation of God the

Creator as far as Eliza is concerned. For her part Eliza will marry. But she won't marry Higgins.

The play ends with Higgins knowingly declaring that Eliza is about to do his shopping for him despite her protestations to the contrary: a statement which actors and critics often take to mean that the pair are a Benedick and Beatrice [from Shakespeare's *Much Ado About Nothing*] who will marry in the end. One need not quote Shaw's own sequel to prove the contrary. The whole point of the great culminating scene is that Eliza has now become not only a person but an independent person. The climax is sharp:

LIZA: If I can't have kindness, I'll have independence.

HIGGINS: Independence? That's middle class blasphemy. We are all dependent on one another, every soul of us on earth.

LIZA: *(rising determinedly)* I'll let you see whether I'm dependent on you. If you can preach, I can teach. I'll go and be a teacher.

HIGGINS: What'll you teach, in heaven's name?

LIZA: What you taught me. I'll teach phonetics.

HIGGINS: Ha! ha! ha!

LIZA: I'll offer myself as an assistant to Professor Nepean.

HIGGINS: *(rising in a fury)* What! That impostor! That humbug! That toadying ignoramus! Teach him *my* methods! *my* discoveries! You take one step in his direction and I'll wring your neck. *(He lays hands on her.)* Do you hear?

LIZA: *(defiantly non-resistant)* Wring away. What do I care? I knew you'd strike me some day. *(He lets her go, stamping with rage. . . .)*

With this cry of victory . . . Eliza wins her freedom. Higgins had said: "I can do without anybody. I have my own soul." And now Eliza can say: "Now . . . I'm not afraid of you and can do without you." After this it does not matter whether Eliza does the shopping or not. The situation is clear. Eliza's fate is settled as far as Higgins is concerned. The story of the experiment is over. Otherwise her fate is as unsettled as yours or mine. This is a true naturalistic ending—not an arbitrary break, but a conclusion which is also a beginning.

THE STRUCTURE OF *PYGMALION*

Pygmalion is a singularly elegant structure. If again we call Act I the prologue, the play falls into two parts of two Acts apiece. Both parts are Pygmalion myths. In the first a duchess is made out of a flower girl. In the second a woman is made out of a duchess. Since these two parts are the main, inner action the omission of the climax of the outer action— the ambassador's reception—will seem particularly discreet,

SHAW'S FASCINATING WOMEN

Eliza Doolitle was only one of a number of strong, independent, fascinating women that George Bernard Shaw created for the stage.

In his plays [George Bernard Shaw] created perhaps the most fascinating gallery of women in modern drama, female characters who usually prove more interesting and more vital than his male characters. His impatience with female stereotypes, although he used them where dramatically valid—and sometimes subconsciously in spite of himself—is everywhere in his writings. In *The Apple Cart,* Orinthia as royal mistress is no longer a sexual vessel but, in effect, a government employee whose "relationship" to the king satisfies the vestigial and vicarious machismo of the populace. In *Heartbreak House,* the husband, not the wife, is kept. In *Pygmalion,* the Cockney flower girl is a human being clever enough to rise by her ability, and, if she chooses, to support a husband rather than fulfill her stereotypic destiny of seeking social and financial security through the prudent bartering of herself in marriage, as her male sponsors Pickering and Higgins recommend. As for romance between Eliza and Higgins, Shaw rejected, from *Pygmalion's* original performance to its being made into a film, any suggestion that there could be a romantic attachment between the "middle-aged bully" and the now beautiful, young flower girl. In *Getting Married,* "Leo" Hotchkiss is not the victim of a mistress-seeking husband; she herself desires a legal, everyday husband and a "Sunday husband" for variety. (As far as marital relations were concerned, Shaw suggested that the public needed "a dose of castor oil" in the form of his plays, and pointed out that his Orinthia-Magnus relationship [in *The Apple Cart*]—a development of "Leo" Hotchkiss's dreams—is an idea Shakespeare had suggested when Beatrice says, [in *Much Ado About Nothing*] in reply to Don Pedro's proposal, "No, my lord, unless I might have another for workingdays: your grace is too costly to wear every day.")

Rodelle Weintraub, ed., *Fabian Feminist: Bernard Shaw and Woman.* University Park: Pennsylvania State University Press, 1977.

economical, and dramatic. The movie version of *Pygmalion* was not the richer for its inclusion. To include a climax that is no climax only blurs the outline of the play. *Pygmalion* is essentially theatrical in construction. It is built in chunks, two by two. The fluidity of the screen is quite inappropriate to it. On the screen, as in the novel, a development of character naturally occurs gradually and smoothly. Natasha in [Russian novelist Leo Tolstoy's] *War and Peace* passes imperceptibly from girlhood to womanhood; Eliza in *Pygmalion* proceeds in dramatically marked stages—one, two, three, four, Act by Act. Perhaps we never realized before the Shaw movies how utterly "of the theatre" the Shaw plays are.

As we might have learned to expect, *Pygmalion* follows the pattern of earlier Shavian works, not duplicating them but following up another aspect of a similar problem. We have seen how the eponymous character is often the representative of vitality and that he remains constant like a catalyst while producing change in others, especially in the antagonist whom he is educating, disillusioning, or converting. *Pygmalion* diverges from the type in that the lifegiver, for all his credentials, and his title of Pygmalion, is suspect. He is not really a life-giver at all. To be sure, Eliza is even more palpably his pupil than Judith was Dick's [in Shaw's *The Devil's Disciple*] or Brassbound Lady Cicely's [in Shaw's *Captain Brassbound's Conversion*]. But the "education of Eliza" in Acts I to III is a caricature of the true process. In the end Eliza turns the tables on Higgins, for she, finally, is the vital one, and he is the prisoner of "system," particularly of his profession.

ALFRED DOOLITTLE'S STORY

Ironically parallel with the story of Eliza is the story of her father. Alfred Doolittle is also suddenly lifted out of slumdom by the caprice of Pygmalion-Higgins. He too has to break bread with dukes and duchesses. Unlike his daughter, however, he is not reborn. He is too far gone for that. He is the same rich as he was poor, the same or worse; for riches carry awful responsibilities, and Doolittle commits the cardinal sin on the Shavian scale—he is irresponsible. In the career of the undeserving poor suddenly become undeserving rich Shaw writes his *social* comedy, his Unpleasant Play, while in the career of his deserving daughter he writes his *human* comedy, his Pleasant Play. Those who think that *Pyg-*

malion is about class society are thinking of Doolittle's comedy rather than Eliza's. The two are carefully related by parallelism and contrast. One might work out an interpretation of the play by comparing their relation to the chief "artificial system" depicted in it—middle-class morality.

A PLAY THAT NEEDS NO DEFENSE

In short, the merit of *Pygmalion* cannot be explained by Shaw's own account of the nature of modern drama, much less by popular or academic opinion concerning Problem Plays, Discussion Drama, Drama of Ideas, and the like. It is a good play by perfectly orthodox standards and needs no theory to defend it. It is Shavian, not in being made up of political or philosophic discussions, but in being based on the standard conflict of vitality and system, in working out this conflict through an inversion of romance, in bringing matters to a head in a battle of wills and words, in having an inner psychological action in counterpoint to the outer romantic action, in existing on two contrasted levels of mentality, both of which are related to the main theme, in delighting and surprising us with a constant flow of verbal music and more than verbal wit.

CHAPTER 3

Themes and Technique

READINGS ON
PYGMALION

A Universal Cinderella Story

Maurice Valency

Despite the play's name, *Pygmalion* does not follow
the Greek myth of Pygmalion and Galatea. Henry
Higgins does not create Eliza; he only revises her. Instead, contends Maurice Valency, the play has more
affinities with the Cinderella fairy tale, a story that
has been especially popular on the Victorian English
stage. The play suggests that Eliza may be only one
of almost limitless educable people of low social
class who may rise in the new society of the twentieth century, in which one's social class is no longer
dictated by birth but is determined by character and
ability. Maurice Valency is the author of the novels
Ashby and *Julie,* and has translated and adapted numerous plays for the stage. His literary criticism includes *Tragedy* and *The Cart and the Trumpet: The
Plays of George Bernard Shaw,* from which this essay is excerpted.

Pygmalion is certainly among the most engaging of Shaw's
plays. It is also among the lightest and most carefree. As the
action is arranged, the question of the ultimate disposition of
the displaced Eliza looms more and more insistently on the
horizon, but from beginning to end Higgins remains bliss-
fully indifferent to the predicament into which his ministra-
tions have placed his protégé and to his own responsibility
for her future. This is the joke upon which the action turns.

As the play progresses, Mrs. Higgins tries to make her son
aware of the seriousness of the situation he is creating, and
Mrs. Pearce, his housekeeper, constantly admonishes him of
the need to think what he is about. Higgins refuses to look
beyond his nose. At the end of the third act, the curtain
speech brings the problem sharply into focus. The expecta-

tion is, therefore, that the situation will be dramatically detonated in the last act, and this is the principal source of suspense in the latter part of the play. In fact nothing of the sort happens. Instead of staging a luxuriously explosive scene ending in a reversal, *Pygmalion* fizzles out in a *Doll's House* [a play by Henrik Ibsen] type of discussion which is never resolved. The play ends, indeed, with the heroine slamming the door on the hero, as in Ibsen's play, but in so deliberate a manner as to warrant the suspicion that the scene is a parody of the celebrated Ibsenist ending.

A CINDERELLA STORY

Doubtless Shaw considered that in deferring the resolution of his plot indefinitely he was following in the footsteps of the master, who also had left the *Doll's House* plot unresolved at the final curtain. But the difference between the two plays is obvious. Ibsen framed his play along the lines of conventional domestic drama, so that his final situation seemed both unusual and shocking. *Pygmalion*, on the other hand, was based on a fairy tale. It is, of course, possible to accord the patterns of myth with the facts of life through the normal methods of symbolism. This is done, for example, in [French writer Jean] Giraudoux's *Ondine,* where the realistic and the mythical are consciously related within a single statement. Naturalism is another matter. It is difficult to imagine anything artistically more inept than a rationalistic conclusion of the Cinderella story. This is, however, precisely what Shaw had in mind in the last act of *Pygmalion.*

By the time *Pygmalion* was written there were in existence innumerable stage versions of Cinderella. The fable offered an excellent basis for plays of *déclassement* [changing one's class]. In all likelihood the direct ancestor of *Pygmalion* was [American playwright Dion] Boucicault's melodrama, *Grimaldi, or the Life of an Actress* (1862), in which a Covent Garden flower-girl is educated, brought to fame, and finally adopted by a broken-down actor, who turns out to be a duke in disguise. Many other analogies have been collected. It seems clear that Shaw intended to follow in *Pygmalion* the traditional formula of such plays—the discovery, the education, the preliminary test, the crucial scene, and so on—up to the point at which the prince and the beggar maid are finally united. Shaw said of the traditional scene of the ball, which *Pygmalion* omits:

The obligatory [necessary; a scene to which the entire plot leads up] scene, the scene in which Eliza makes her successful début at the Ambassador's party, was the root of the play at its inception. But when I got to work I left it to the imagination of the audience, as the theatre could not afford the expense, and it made the play too long. Sir James Barrie spotted this at once and remonstrated. So when the play was screened, I added the omitted scene.

The scene of the ball which Shaw added to the screen version of the play was not, however, obligatory. It was merely decorative. A love scene at the end of the play was really obligatory. It was therefore regularly supplied by the actors from the time of Beerbohm Tree, in the teeth of the author's peremptory instructions to the contrary. The discussion which, in the fifth act, serves the purpose of a denouement therefore constitutes a serious embarrassment in the development of the action. This scene . . . advances the plot not a jot further than the fourth-act curtain and is therefore both superfluous and repetitious. It is in any case quite irrelevant to an anecdote which admits of only one acceptable solution.

A myth is ordinarily an organism of very precise form. Such durable fantasies come into being as the result of a subtle interplay of psychic forces and are in every case living things carefully designed to subserve a necessary function. For this reason, myths, like trees, are constructs of limited elasticity, and any serious attempt to distort their structure will encounter resistance. No application of logic will serve to transform the myth of Cinderella into anything other than what it is. Once the fairy godmother has waved her wand and the girl's magical transformation has been effected, it is absolutely indispensable that the Prince should seek out the resulting Princess, marry her, and live happily with her forever after.

In fact, Shaw was too canny a writer to spoil his play by tampering with the vital elements of the fairy tale. It is reasonably clear in the third act that Higgins, for all his protestations, is in the toils of the Life Force, very much as [Shaw's character] Tanner is in *Man and Superman,* that he would rather die than part with Eliza, and that she is destined to live with him, more or less happily, all the rest of his life in the flat in Wimpole Street. In this regard the play is neither perverse nor inept. The epilogue is another matter.

The epilogue is a prose narrative, offered provisionally for the edification of those who insist on having the story resolved. From every point of view the proposed resolution is unsatisfactory; nevertheless it indicates a good deal about Shaw's attitude toward his characters and his play and thus affords some insight into the influences which gave the play its shape. In the epilogue it is demonstrated that Higgins belongs to the category of the unmarriageable . . . whose destiny it is to produce ideas, but not children. The demonstration depends, of course, on the depiction of Higgins as a cranky and egotistical genius, whose good qualities do not include a capacity for sympathy. As Shaw portrays him, Higgins is not lovable; he is overwhelming. His single-mindedness is impressive, and it is amusing, but it is not an endearing trait. The normal expectation is that the author will manage his redemption through love. He does not. From beginning to end, his hero is as hard as nails, a sacrificial offering to the cause of realism. . . .

CASTE IS CHARACTER AND ABILITY

On the question of caste the play is clearer in its doctrine. Shaw assigns to each individual his exact specific gravity in the social order. In the epilogue to *Pygmalion* the Eynsford-Hills, who cling desperately to their upper-class status in spite of their poverty, are brought down to the level of small shopkeepers. In the play itself Eliza is accepted by Mrs. Higgins as a social equal; but Higgins is willing to accept her as such only when she indicates her potentialities as a professional competitor. The astonishing rise of Mr. Doolittle is . . . somewhat more improbable than the other improbabilities of the play: it is this sort of imaginative leap that causes so much of Shaw's comedy to approximate extravaganza. But, however unrealistic they may be, these unexpected reversals are refreshing, and certainly they serve a useful function. For Shaw caste is essentially a matter of character and ability, not of birth, so that once the individual is cut free of the restrictions of class, he tends to find his own level in the human hierarchy. Social mobility is indispensable to the evolutionary process.

While such is, beyond doubt, the conclusion to be drawn from the play, the epilogue suggests a contrary inference. Here Shaw declined to imagine the easy rise of his gifted heroine, even as the owner of a flower shop. On the contrary, he found it necessary, in the name of realism, to punish Eliza and her hapless spouse, Freddy Hill, by putting them through an obstacle course of economic vicissitudes as arduous as his own had been before fortune favored him.

The proposed solution of Eliza's economic problem therefore seems dismally novelistic. Experience indicates that in reality beautiful girls of exceptional ability do not marry impecunious Freddies. They marry industrial magnates of a certain age and are eventually widowed or divorced with stupendous financial settlements. The meager destiny which Shaw metes out to his Galatea [the statue in the Pygmalion myth] in the name of realism must therefore be accounted an unpardonable intrusion of common sense not only upon the myth but also upon that aspect of the myth which is normally thought of as reality.

CINDERELLA MUST HAVE HER PRINCE

In fact, the mythological pattern which includes such stories as *The Ugly Duckling, Cinderella, Beauty and the Beast, King Cophetua and the Beggar Maid,* and *The Patient Griselda*—all of which depend on the ultimate recognition of the superior merits of a disprized individual—is a compensatory mechanism of the greatest efficacy in the management of feelings of inferiority. For this reason, if no other, it is indispensable that Cinderella have her prince at the end of her story, and any other culmination is in the nature of a betrayal. Happily, Shaw had the good sense to leave the way open in his play for an inference of fulfillment according to the rules of romance, and *Pygmalion* has always been played in this manner. In the end, in spite of the author, Jack has his Jill. The epilogue may therefore be dismissed as an unfortunate irrelevancy, interesting chiefly because of the insight it affords into the mentality of the author.

The myth upon which *Pygmalion* is based has, of course, nothing to do with the legend of Pygmalion and Galatea. The Pygmalion story was treated most perceptively by [Italian playwright Luigi] Pirandello in *Diana e la Tuda* (1927) fourteen years after Shaw's play was written, and it had already furnished the basis for Ibsen's *When We Dead Awaken* (1899) fourteen years before. It is possible that Shaw had Ibsen's play in mind in devising *Pygmalion,* but the relation is not very close. Higgins does not create Eliza. He merely revises her. His relation to her is not artistic, but surgical. In *When We Dead Awaken,* the sculptor Rubek is destroyed because he has preferred his creation to the living woman who informed it, and toward the end of his life he realizes with regret that in his eagerness to work he has forgotten to live. Higgins has no such difficulty. For him work and life are synonymous. He has no need of love and is quite willing to sacrifice Eliza to his career, though he obviously finds her presence more convenient than her absence.

SHAW'S COMEDIES AND IBSEN'S TRAGEDIES

The final scene of *Pygmalion* is in some sense a realization of the scene—which in *When We Dead Awaken* Ibsen forbore to write—in which Rubek lets Irene go after he has finished with her as a model. For Irene the epilogue is prostitution and afterwards madness. For Rubek it is disillusion, regret, and eventually death. But in *Pygmalion* Eliza parts company with Higgins long before any of these operatic developments take place. Eliza may or may not look after Higgins's shopping list after the final curtain. It is no great matter: the sequel is not likely to be tragic. . . . Ibsen's heroes invariably live to regret their single-minded dedication to their vocation. Shaw's heroes revel in it.

Ibsen came to the conclusion relatively early in his career that the sense of vocation is a special form of madness, and that life is justified mainly by love. Shaw thought of love as a physical urge which must at all costs be prevented from interfering with a creative man's work, in which chiefly his salvation lies. The two viewpoints are diametrically opposed and reflect the profound difference in temperament between the master and his foremost disciple in the drama. In Ibsen's plays, characters like Higgins are monomaniacs who come invariably to a tragic end. Shaw, however, found his professor singularly congenial, and he gave him a distinctly comic turn.

ON HENRY HIGGINS

In Higgins we are invited to see more of [English linguist and the model for Higgins] Henry Sweet than of Shaw, but he has a good deal of Shaw's shamelessness, his impudence, and his gift of blarney. There is, moreover, something ungainly in Higgins's insistence on the virtues of the intellectual life. He tells Eliza:

> If you cant stand the coldness of my sort of life, and the strain of it, go back to the gutter. Work til you are more a brute than a human being; and then cuddle and squabble and drink til you fall asleep. Oh, it's a fine life, the life of the gutter. It's real:

it's warm: it's violent: you can feel it through the thickest skin: you can taste it and smell it without any training or any work. Not like Science and Literature and Classical Music and Philosophy and Art. You find me cold, unfeeling, selfish, dont you? Very well: be off with you to the sort of people you like. Marry some sentimental hog or other with lots of money, and a thick pair of lips to kiss you with and a thick pair of boots to kick you with. If you cant appreciate what youve got, youd better get what you can appreciate.

In such passages one uncomfortably senses the intellectual snob. It would be charitable to suppose that Shaw expressed through Higgins not his own intellectual smugness, but what he imagined a character like Higgins might feel, but there are too many echoes of this attitude in Shaw's personal correspondence to make the supposition likely. In any case the passage is unfortunate, and confirms one's opinion that Higgins is not a particularly pleasant man. Even for a stage professor, he seems relatively bloodless. . . . Nevertheless Higgins's desperate search for Eliza in the last act, his manifest jealousy of Freddy, and his exaggerated posturings in the final scene suggest that he feels some emotional need for the girl he so scornfully rejected, and that ultimately he means to get her, like an astute man of business, on his own terms.

As Shaw describes him, Higgins comically suggests madness. He considers himself to be a modest, diffident, shy, and soft-spoken man of irreproachable manners. He is in fact a brash and tyrannical egotist, generous, but rude and totally inconsiderate of others. Evidently Shaw found this type of superman a little awesome. In his epilogue he says of Eliza that she may sometimes imagine

> Higgins making love like any common man. . . . But when it comes to business, to the life that she really leads as distinguished from the life of dreams and fancies, she likes Freddy and she likes the Colonel; and she does not like Higgins and Mr. Doolittle. Galatea never does quite like Pygmalion: his relation to her is too godlike to be altogether agreeable.

A PERFECT MOTHER SETS A HIGH STANDARD

This observation, though witty, belies the play. If Eliza did not find Higgins likeable she could have no real emotional involvement with him, and the contrast which Shaw meant to dramatize between her romantic illusions and his cold realism could not be demonstrated. One may wonder why Shaw found it so necessary to stress Higgins's aversion from sexual involvements with so attractive a girl as Eliza.

His reasons are interesting:

> When Higgins excused his indifference to young women on
> the ground that they had an irresistible rival in his mother, he
> gave the clue to his inveterate old-bachelordom. The case is
> uncommon only to the extent that remarkable mothers are
> uncommon. If an imaginative boy has a sufficiently rich
> mother who has intelligence, personal grace, dignity of char-
> acter without harshness, and a cultivated sense of the best art
> of her time to enable her to make her house beautiful, she
> sets a standard for him against which very few women can
> struggle, besides effecting for him a disengagement of his af-
> fections, his sense of beauty, and his idealism from his specif-
> ically sexual impulses. This makes him a standing puzzle to
> the huge number of uncultivated people who have been
> brought up in tasteless homes by commonplace or disagree-
> able parents, and to whom, consequently, literature, painting,
> sculpture, music and affectionate personal relations come as
> modes of sex if they come at all. . . .

Shaw thus introduced into the Higgins-Eliza discussion
what appears to be a deeply personal note. Mrs. Higgins is a
personification of the ideal mother according to Shaw—a
beautiful woman, charming, intelligent, and rich. She is a
person of impeccable taste. Her apartment is described in detail. It is spacious, uncluttered, and decorated in accordance
with the best pre-Raphaelite standards. They contrast
sharply with the Victorian jumble to which her son is committed. Mrs. Higgins wisely keeps him at some distance, but
there is no doubt that she finds him amusing as well as ex-
asperating, and she manages him adroitly like a willful child.
There is no suggestion in the play of any sort of rivalry between Mrs. Higgins and Eliza. It is suggested, on the contrary,
that she would make the most desirable of mothers-in-law.

The rationalization of Higgins's sexlessness in the epilogue was in all likelihood an afterthought, but it has the advantage of affording us another glimpse of the motives
which underlie the play. Shaw's dependence on his mother
during the early part of his life, and her habitual indifference to his concerns, were . . . amply reflected in his early
novels. It is easy to discern in these fantasies the injury to his
ego which her indifference caused him, and it is even possible to perceive, if we wish, something of the sort in several
of the early plays, particularly in *Mrs. Warren's Profession.* . . .

In *Pygmalion* there is nothing to suggest that Higgins is a
socialist, and he has apparently no idea of leveling the
classes under a common phonetic system. But the implica-

tion is that what could be done with Eliza Doolittle can be done, more or less successfully, with anyone who shows the necessary aptitude. Shaw himself had learned upper-class English ways in somewhat the same manner as Eliza, and he evidently liked the idea that in order to transform a clever garbageman into a prime minister all that is necessary is a course in speech. Such ideas were certainly current in the early decades of [the twentieth] century, and the vast proliferation of speech courses in those years attests to the influence of the theory.

Eliza observes very justly that what makes a lady is the manner in which she is treated. The idea that all those who make estimable sounds will be treated as ladies and gentlemen, so that socialism will spring up by itself . . . depends, however, upon a strictly Victorian concept of the hierarchy of classes. In the 1870's, possibly, Higgins might feel some sense of the futility of his profession; but in 1913 he has the professional ardor of a true revolutionist. He tells his mother: "you have no idea how frightfully interesting it is to take a human being and change her into a quite different human being by creating a new speech for her. It's filling up the deepest gulf that separates class from class and soul from soul."

The suggestion that, if Eliza behaves like a duchess, she may well become a duchess is—however one calculates the probabilities—immediately acceptable in the theater. Consequently the intermediate stages in the assumption of Eliza are fascinating. The incongruity between what Eliza says at Mrs. Higgins's at-home, and the manner in which she says it, provided Mrs. Pat Campbell [the actress who first played Eliza on the London stage] with an incomparable opportunity to display her comic talents, and the effect of Eliza's elegant rendition of "Not bloody likely" is said to have been the talk of London all during the first run of the play. Clara Hill, on the other hand, illustrates a tendency contrary to that which motivates Eliza's rise in the world. She is quite ready to affect lower-class speech patterns if they are considered fashionable. In Shaw's day the attrition of the King's English was evidently already a cause for concern:

> PICKERING: . . . Ive been away in India for several years, and manners have changed so much that I sometimes dont know whether I'm at a respectable dinnertable or in a ship's forecastle.

CLARA: It's all a matter of habit. Theres no right or wrong in it. Nobody means anything by it and it's so quaint, and gives such a smart emphasis to things that are not in themselves very witty. I find the new small talk delightful and quite innocent.

A CLASSLESS SOCIETY

Possibly for Shaw these indications of the tendency to obliterate class distinctions presaged the classless society of the future, but it is more likely that he saw in this process a salutary movement of individuals to take their proper places in the social hierarchy regardless of the class into which they were born. *Pygmalion* is a play of exceptional people. Eliza, like her father, is a highly evolved individual whose potentialities would normally be stifled by the limitations of a rigidly stratified social environment. But even when she is artificially freed from the restrictions of her social class, her economic possibilities are a matter of chance. . . . Mr. Doolittle, on the other hand, is emancipated not by education but by money, with the result that he joins the middle class and is cursed with the need for respectability all the rest of his life.

The intimation is that social displacement is both perilous and uncomfortable no matter how it is brought about: nevertheless it is indispensable to the evolution of society. In *Pygmalion* it is accident that determines the extraordinary rise of Eliza and her father; but the rapid development of mass education in England in this period was already making it possible for the underprivileged to become privileged as a matter of course. What *Pygmalion* describes is the process by which exceptional people find their way into the upper reaches of society, and from this point of view it is perhaps a satire. But its satirical intention does not obscure the underlying idea. The evolutionary principle involves a constant displacement of individuals within the class structure. The result is doubtless of benefit to the species, but it is not uniformly pleasant for the individual. . . . *Pygmalion* . . . is very funny; but it too has its pathetic side. Nature is insensible to suffering. Its obtuseness is mirrored in the insensitivity of Higgins, who identifies with nobody and is therefore inhuman to a degree that is not altogether agreeable. But the fact is that Eliza, as she repeatedly points out, has her feelings like any one else; and it is in keeping this poignant consideration constantly before his audience that Shaw, for all his realism, shows his worth as a dramatist.

Pygmalion as a Transformation Myth

Timothy G. Vesonder

Audiences who prefer the romantic ending that was added to *Pygmalion* by other play producers have been confused by the play's conflicting mythologies. Both the Pygmalion myth and the Cinderella tale end in marriage, as does the traditional comic ending. But *Pygmalion* is not so much about these paradigms as it is a transformation tale, argues Timothy G. Vesonder. In the manner of Ovid's mythological tales, Eliza's story is that of a transformed creature. The transformation tale allows people to use their imagination to gain some measure of control over a world that may be alien or even hostile. If Eliza returns to Henry, she would have to remain subservient, which contradicts the nature of the transformation tale. Instead, she gains a measure of control by rejecting Higgins's proposal for a life of her own. Timothy G. Vesonder has taught at Pennsylvania State University, Shenango Valley.

In writing *Pygmalion,* Shaw borrowed and adapted many myths which led, rather inevitably, to confusion over the last moments of the play. Unable to identify the controlling mythic pattern, actors as well as audiences were unprepared for and unsatisfied with the feminist thrust of Eliza's decision to leave Higgins. The first as well as the most influential of the misled was Beerbohm Tree, the Henry Higgins of the play's London premiere. Tree ignored Shaw's instructions and at the end of every performance threw flowers to Mrs. Patrick Campbell (Eliza Doolittle), suggesting a romantic attachment that would end in marriage. When Shaw complained, the actor wrote to him: "My ending makes money: you ought to be grateful." Shaw countered: "Your

Excerpted from "Eliza's Choice: Transformation Myth and the Ending of *Pygmalion*," by Timothy G. Vesonder, in *Fabian Feminist: Bernard Shaw and Woman,* edited by Rodelle Weintraub (University Park: Pennsylvania State University Press, 1977). Copyright © 1977 by Rodelle Weintraub. Reprinted with permission.

ending is damnable: you ought to be shot."

Generally, audiences preferred the more romantic ending of Tree's interpretation; and Shaw could not convert them from this error even with his prose epilogue, which he published in 1915 to prove that Eliza married Freddy and remained only a friend to Higgins. In 1938, ignoring both the epilogue and Shaw's film script, Gabriel Pascal gave movie audiences an ending similar to Tree's, in that a seemingly docile Eliza returned to Higgins. Shaw had died before the production of the musical adaptation of the play, *My Fair Lady,* but even had he been alive, it is unlikely that he could have changed the then familiar romantic finale. Actors, audiences and producers were joined by many critics who also favored the revised ending. In [his] book on Shaw's work, Maurice Valency even argued that Eliza and Higgins would make an ideal couple, and that the Shaw ending is dramatically unsatisfying and unacceptable.

Conflicting Myths

Rarely has an author's intention been so ignored or a classic work so mistreated. However unfortunate, the misinterpretations of *Pygmalion* are understandable when we recognize that the confusion comes largely from the conflicting myths which Shaw used in the play. The most obvious mythic source is underlined by the title. Henry Higgins's re-creation of Eliza Doolittle parallels many details of the Greek myth in which an artist, Pygmalion, disenchanted with the women around him, sculpts a statue of his ideal woman. The artist falls in love with his creation and prays to Aphrodite to give his ivory maiden life. When the lover's plea is answered, Pygmalion marries his creation. Along with the Greek myth, Shaw's *Pygmalion* also contains many elements of the Cinderella folk tale. Just as the poor and mistreated Cinderella becomes a princess through the intervention of her fairy godmother, Shaw's flower girl is elevated briefly into the aristocracy and permanently into the middle class.

A crucial difference between these stories and Shaw's play is that Eliza does not marry Henry Higgins at the end of the play, nor does she continue to live with him as servant, secretary, and protégée, the roles Higgins wants her to play. In the last scene, Eliza announces that she wants more out of life than the companionship Higgins offers her, and she threatens to marry Freddy Hill. Remembering, at least subconsciously, that the Pygmalion myth and the Cinderella folk tale end in the marriage of the principal characters, audiences expect Shaw to end his play similarly.

Despite the expectations of its audiences, Shaw's intention for the ending of *Pygmalion* is quite clear. Historically, Shaw's argument with Tree, his epilogue and his movie script solidly confirm his original ending. Textually, no line or stage direction even remotely suggests that Eliza will choose Higgins over Freddy. Realistically, as Shaw explains in the epilogue, Eliza cannot marry Higgins. True, they are both very charming, very bright and very strong characters who engage our affection and admiration; and the match-making part in all of us wants to see these two likeable personalities joined in lasting connubial bliss. But common sense should tell us otherwise. Higgins, after all, is a confirmed bachelor who can love only one woman, his mother; but even mother and son find life under the same roof—if for only a few hours at a time—intolerable. Higgins wants his independence and his work; Eliza wants her independence and affection. A compromise between these strong characters is as unlikely as it is undesirable.

SHAW'S LOVE OF IRONY

Dramatically, *Pygmalion* repeats patterns and techniques that Shaw used consistently in his earlier plays. He delighted in irony, especially in denying audience expectations by inverting material. A Pygmalion who does not marry his creation is a rather mild departure from the expected, compared to many previous Shavian ironies, such as a hero who retreats, a minister who turns revolutionary, a world conqueror who abhors violence, a Don Juan who is pursued by a woman, and a doctor who kills. Eliza also is typical of many of Shaw's female characters. By leaving Higgins, she joins a long line of Shaw women who reject marriage to likely candidates. . . .

THE COMIC CONVENTION OF MARRIAGE

Despite the strength of these arguments, many still wishfully push Higgins and Eliza toward marriage, and in so doing they are imposing the conventions of archetypal comedy on the structure of *Pygmalion*. In the archetypal comic plot, blocking characters and obstacles are overcome by the lovers, whose marriage at the end of the play signals the rec-

onciliation and renewal of their society. Although this comic
convention enjoys great popular appeal, it is wrong to apply
it to a Shaw play which does not show a man and a woman
hurdling obstacle after obstacle to land finally in each
other's arms. Such is the case in *Arms and the Man* and *You
Never Can Tell*, but in *Pygmalion* the two marriages that do
figure in the closing scene are incidental and not important
in themselves.

THE HEROIC ARCHETYPE

To find the mythic model for *Pygmalion* we must look beyond the conventions of comedy with its devices of trickery,
deceit and coincidence to the conventions of archetypal romance. The structure of this archetype is built around the
hero, the possessor of great power which he attains from his
semidivine birth or from divine favor. With this great power
the hero performs wondrous deeds, defeats evil forces and
thereby insures the well-being of his society.

Even a superficial examination of *Pygmalion* will show
that the main focus of the play is not erotic involvement but
the power of language and that Henry Higgins is much more
the hero than the lover. Shaw's story, simply stated, portrays
an expert linguist who accepts a challenge to re-create a
poor, uneducated young woman by teaching her how to
speak properly. Linguistic knowledge and skills are the
great weapons which Higgins uses to defeat evil and improve society. When he first meets Eliza, he notes that her
kerbstone English will keep her in the gutter. She is in the
clutches of the monster of poverty, which was to Shaw the
greatest modern demon. Higgins cannot kill this monster,
but he can use his powers to free Eliza from its grip. Just as
the classical hero received help from gods, friends and
benevolent spirits, the Shavian hero receives necessary assistance from his mother and from Colonel Pickering. Higgins supplies the technical skill and the discipline, but his
assistants give Eliza the necessary qualities of common
sense and humanity.

Even if we see *Pygmalion* in the pattern of archetypal romance, the problem with the ending remains, for the hero
often receives a woman as the reward of his labors at the
culmination of his quest. Just as Perseus has his Andromeda
and Sigurd his Brynhild, it is mythically consistent that Higgins should have his Eliza. Their marriage, however, is not

a necessity, for in myth celibacy also has its models in many gods, the forerunners of the heroes, who do not take mates. Often those divinities most involved in the lives of men, such as Athena, Artemis, Apollo and Dionysus, avoid marriage to devote themselves to their missions. Recalling the stories of Theseus and Ariadne and of Aeneas and Dido, we can see that even heroes do not always leap into marriage with the first likely candidate.

Apart from these mythic precedents, we can understand and defend the changes Shaw makes in the archetypal romance if we acknowledge the theory of displacement, which holds that a writer will make changes in a myth to make his story more realistic, more credible to his audience. Thus, Higgins does not go on a long and perilous journey looking for monsters to kill; nor does he have a magic sword or shield or a protecting deity hovering over him. As a displaced hero, Higgins is devoted to science, which is a modern quest to improve life, to rid the world of weakness and evil. His powerful weapon is his linguisitic expertise, which he uses in his quest to make earth a little more like heaven, "where there are no third-class carriages, and one soul is as good as another," where all men are treated equally. In his quest the modern hero does not always want or need the fulfillment of marriage, and the modern maiden, more independent than her classical counterparts, may ignore the savior whose ideals she does not share. In the mythic retelling, then, Eliza may leave Higgins and marry Freddy, and Higgins, having freed his Andromeda from a living death, can move on to further adventures.

A Transformation Story

The most satisfying mythic understanding of the Shaw ending does not come from an examination of Higgins as hero or of *Pygmalion* as romance. Although the play is the story of a modern hero with modern powers, it is likewise the story of the effect of these powers, a story not only of liberation but also of transformation.

Eliza begins the play as a poor flower girl who is ignored by Freddy Hill and family and is easily intimidated by Higgins. With much work and the help of Higgins and company she begins to change. Her success at the Embassy Ball marks one stage in her growth, but it is hardly the climax or the great victory that the film-makers would have us believe.

It is after the ball that Eliza shows her new powers: she has charm enough to keep a man, who in Act I never noticed her, at a constant vigil near her doorstep, and she has money enough to secure a cab to drive about in all night, an experience that was impossible for the flower girl. Most importantly, Eliza shows her new strength and independence when she walks out on Higgins, a decision that she confirms in the final scene. Here Eliza explains to Higgins that she doesn't want to live in his house and be treated as a maid or a personal secretary. She doesn't want to be treated as an equal, as "one of the boys," the way Higgins treats everyone he respects. She has no interest in the "higher life." Eliza does want "a little kindness," the simple love and affection that a Freddy Hill can supply. This revelation upsets Higgins, who tries to bully Eliza into submission. At this point, the real climax of the play, Eliza shows that she is no longer the flower girl who was tempted by chocolates or intimidated by threats. Announcing that she is as good as he is, that she has her own dreams and ideals, Eliza firmly establishes her independence. Higgins himself is forced to admit that she can make it without him and that he will miss her. He is forced to admit that she is finally a total person—her transformation is complete.

That the last act of *Pygmalion* does not emphasize marriage is reinforced by the reappearance of Alfred Doolittle. The dustman too has been transformed with the help of Higgins. The poor worker with few obligations has become the middle-class lecturer with many responsibilities. His impending marriage, unimportant in itself, is another indication of the drastic change in his life style. Doolittle himself is basically the same character: his change is largely economic. In contrast, Eliza's change is largely spiritual: she is a new person inside and out.

The transformations we see in the last act of *Pygmalion* are a basic mythic motif. An obvious and predominant pattern in Ovid's *Metamorphoses,* transformations occur so often in myths and in folk tales that they seem to be a basic exercise of man's imaginative powers. In trying to explain this common theme, Northrop Frye suggests that man, by virtue of his imagination, can gain some control over a world which is alien and often hostile. In his imagination man can re-create the world or at least understand its mysteries, which is another form of control. He can change the sun into a god, a god into a man, or a man into a constellation. He can change a statue into a living woman, a poor girl into a princess, and a flower girl into a "consort battleship." The core of the Pygmalion myth and of the Cinderella folk tale is the transformation, not the marriage: while Shaw does not use his sources as a prescription for his plot, he does preserve the fundamental pattern common to both stories. In this sense, he does not invert the myths so much as he retells them.

ELIZA'S TRIUMPH

From this perspective we can understand why Shaw would be so concerned by the productions which hinted at a deeper attachment between Eliza and Higgins. If Eliza remains with Higgins, in mythic terms, the hero would receive his reward, and Eliza would have to submit herself to her savior. This, in fact, was probably the ideal that animated many of those who wanted Eliza to remain with Higgins: the submissive woman, fetching slippers and managing the household, while the eccentric hero tends to higher affairs. What these revisionists failed to see is that in their ending Eliza only would trade masters—poverty and vulgarity for Higgins—and her own transformation would not be as deep or as dramatic.

In effect, the popular interpretation changes the focus of the ending: it elevates Higgins and reduces Eliza; it emphasizes the hero over his work, the transformer over the transformation, one myth over another. On the other hand, when we recognize the play as a retelling of an archetypal transformation, we can see that Shaw gave the first part of the play to Higgins but reserved the last for Eliza. She was not to be a reward for the hero, slipper-fetcher and house manager. The flower girl was changed into a strong and independent woman—a woman equal to the hero. Joining the ranks of the other strong female characters such as Vivie Warren, Candida Morell, Ann Whitefield, Barbara Undershaft and Lina Szczepanowska, Eliza Doolittle stands up to Higgins and thus takes an active role in deciding her own destiny. Although we may respect and applaud Higgins's powers, in the end the triumph is Eliza's, and the greatest applause should be reserved for the new woman, Shaw's modern Galatea and twentieth-century Cinderella.

Doolittle's Comic Language Suggests More Serious Themes

John A. Mills

Shaw creates comedy through Alfred Doolittle's manner of speech, which often contrasts slang words and formal language in the same sentence. But Shaw has a more serious purpose, according to John A. Mills. Doolittle's character is a mixture of high and low, of serious, even intellectual thought contrasted with questionable morals. His vulgarity of speech parallels his vulgarity of taste, and his refined diction reveals an ability to function on higher planes of thought. Mills has taught at Indiana University and the State University of New York at Binghamton.

Alfred [Doolittle] provokes laughter by his frequent employment of a speech style all out of keeping with the lowliness of his vowels and consonants. The neat rhetorical turn of his "I'm willing to tell you. I'm wanting to tell you. I'm waiting to tell you," unlooked for in the mouth of a "common dustman," easily arouses the amused admiration of Higgins and can hardly fail to delight the audience as well.

MIXING SLANG AND FORMAL LANGUAGE

More often than not, his polished phrases collide not only with his phonetic distortions, but also with other elements of the vernacular, especially slang words and expressions, as in: "I can't carry the girl through the streets like a bloomin monkey, can I? I put it to you." Here the formal ring of "I put it to you," a phrase common to legal debate, sounds ludicrous beside the homely "bloomin monkey." In another speech, he strides imperiously through a nicely balanced parallelism, only to butt square against a barbarism of grammar: "Just one good spree for myself and the missus, giving

Excerpted from *Language and Laughter: Comic Diction in the Plays of Bernard Shaw*, by John A. Mills. Copyright © 1969 The Arizona Board of Regents. Reprinted by permission of the University of Arizona Press.

pleasure to ourselves and employment to others, and satisfaction to you to think it's not been throwed away." In his "What am I, Governors both?" he takes the familiar cockney term of address "Governor," converts it to a very mannered plural, and uses it in that perennial of florid oratory, the rhetorical question.

The most pronounced and most delightful example of this tendency is Alfred's persistent sporting with the phrase "deserving poor," that indispensible shibboleth [a common phrase] of the professionally charitable. Having decided that he belongs to the "*un*deserving poor," he frequently enlarges on the subject, pointing out the drawbacks of such a condition but admitting that it holds a certain attraction for him. "Undeserving poverty is my line," he avows. "Taking one station in society with another, it's—it's—well, it's the only one that has any ginger in it, to my taste."

In a similar fashion, he rather handily tosses about the phrase "middle-class morality," which he defines as "an excuse never to give [him] anything." When he comes into the Wannafeller Pre-digested Cheese annuity, he accuses Higgins of having "tied me up and delivered me into the hands of middle-class morality." Deploring the fact that, as a man of means, he will now have to support his relatives and friends, he concludes: "I have to live for others and not for myself: that's middle-class morality."

These rhetorical flourishes, comic by contrast with the vulgarisms of diction which house them, seem to be part and parcel of the comic essence of Doolittle's character, rather than mere laughter-provoking devices gratuitously superimposed. For Doolittle, as he himself explicitly asserts on at least three separate occasions, is a "thinking man." He substantiates this claim to a certain refinement of intellectual perception by the quality of thinking he reveals in his various exchanges with Higgins and Pickering. Witness his shrewd analysis of his relations with his current "companion": "I'm willing [to marry her]. It's me that suffers by it. I've no hold on her. I got to buy her clothes something sinful. I'm a slave to that woman, Governor, just because I'm not her lawful husband. And she knows it too. Catch her marrying me!" Higgins also lends authority to the claim by avowing that with three months' speech training behind him, Doolittle "could choose between a seat in the Cabinet and a popular pulpit in Wales."

This intellectual agility of Doolittle's, so amply evidenced in the play, seems to form the very core of his comic being. The juxtaposition of his better-than-average, if not superior, intellectual qualifications, with his questionable moral qualifications—as evidenced in his laziness, fondness for drink, etc.,—produces a richly comic portrait. In fact, it is precisely this imbalance of natural proclivities which generates his comic dilemma; his irrepressible cleverness trips him up first by denying him a place in the ranks of the "deserving poor," and finally by bringing about that most dreaded calamity, his elevation to the middle class.

If this analysis of Doolittle's character and situation is correct, then his habits of speech may be seen to have an organic relationship with them. Just as the mental and moral

---

SHAW'S DECISION NOT TO USE DIALECT THROUGHOUT *PYGMALION*

A critic explains why, after only one speech, Shaw abandoned his attempt to phonetically transcribe Eliza's cockney accent.

With Shaw's lifelong interest in dialect and phonetics, it was inevitable that he should write *Pygmalion,* in which a cockney flower-girl is turned into a lady by a phonetician who teaches her to speak correctly. The odd circumstance is that after one short speech of Liza's, written phonetically, Shaw says in a stage direction: "Here, with apologies, this desperate attempt to represent her dialect without a phonetic alphabet must be abandoned as unintelligible outside London." Evidently Liza's case convinced him, as those of Burgess, Drinkwater, the cockneys in *Major Barbara* [in Shaw's other plays], and others had not, that elaborate attempts to represent dialect accurately are impracticable. The admission does not specifically extend to the spoken dialect in the theatre, but probably Shaw recognized that an exact reproduction of Liza's speech would be as unintelligible to hearers outside of London as to readers. His previous experiments had been with secondary characters, whose queer noises might be amusing even if not understood; but Liza, as the heroine, must be fairly intelligible. The cockney part of the role presents a difficult problem to the actress, and Shaw tacitly admits that the solution must be turned over to her and to the director.

Homer E. Woodbridge, *George Bernard Shaw: Creative Artist.* Carbondale: Southern Illinois University Press, 1963.

aspects of his character jostle each other in comic incongruity, so do the stylistic and phonetic components of his speech; vulgarity of speech-sound parallels vulgarity of taste, while refinement of word-choice and arrangement parallels refinement of thought. Some such close connection between style of speaking and style of living seems substantiated, moreover, by a particularly significant revelation Doolittle makes to Higgins shortly after his first appearance. "Ive heard all the preachers and all the prime ministers—for I'm a thinking man and game for politics or religion or social reform same as all the other amusements—. . . ." The speech not only gives further evidence of his ability to function on the higher planes of thought, but also reveals the source of his turn for oratorical niceties of expression.

The Deeper Meaning Behind Shaw's Funniest Scene

Leon Hugo

Leon Hugo suggests that the most amusing scene in all of Shaw's work occurs when the new, proper Eliza is introduced to polite society in Mrs. Higgins's drawing room. Eliza's precise upper-class accent clashes with her lower-class content to create richly comic dialogue. But behind the comedy, Shaw points to the great gap between social classes that allows this scene to be funny. The chasm between the wealthy and the poor that fuels the comedy in this scene is ultimately a satiric commentary on a society that promotes such social distance. Leon Hugo has taught at the University of South Africa. His books include *Edwardian Shaw: The Writer and His Age* and *Bernard Shaw: Playwright and Preacher*, from which this article is excerpted.

We may . . . pluck from that comparatively slight but incandescent play, *Pygmalion*, the scene which is probably the most explosively amusing in the entire body of Shaw's work: Liza Doolittle's introduction into polite society. We may take the delight of the scene for granted and limit ourselves to considering why we laugh and what Shavian purpose underlies the laughter.

Liza enters Mrs Higgins's drawing-room and everyone, not excepting members of the audience, who have last seen her in her Lissom Grove finery, is stunned. As Shaw says, she creates an impression of remarkable distinction and beauty. She greets everybody in the most perfectly articulated English. She seats herself in a graceful and easy—in a completely lady-like—manner. Then:

MRS HIGGINS: *(at last, conversationally)* Will it rain, do you think?

LIZA: The shallow depression in the west of these islands is likely to move slowly in an easterly direction. There are no indications of any great change in the barometrical situation.

A MISALLIANCE OF MATTER AND MANNER

And Freddy laughs and we laugh. Why? Freddy because he thinks this an example of the new 'small talk' and the quintessence of drawing room wit, we because Liza's remark is so absurdly inappropriate to the polite conventions of an 'at home'. As we know, this absurdity is very shortly to swell to sheer grotesquerie when Liza embarks on her history:

LIZA: *(darkly)* My aunt died of influenza: so they said. . . . But its my belief they done the old woman in.

MRS HIGGINS: *(puzzled)* Done her in?

LIZA: Y—e—e—e-es, Lord love you! Why should she die of influenza? She come through diphtheria right enough the year before. I saw her with my own eyes. Fairly blue with it, she was. They all thought she was dead; but my father he kept ladling gin down her throat til she came to so sudden that she bit the bowl off the spoon. . . .

By now the marriage between manner and matter is not merely inappropriate: it is a fantastic misalliance. And Freddy laughs and we laugh so uproariously that we may quite possibly not listen to Mrs Eynsford Hill's words. She, plaintively ineffectual lady that she is, mentally, emotionally, and socially equipped to see as far as her own genteel distress but no further, accepts this Miss Doolittle on drawing-room terms—and so, of course, finds herself appalled and bewildered by the matter-of-factness of Lissom Grove.

MRS EYNSFORD HILL: *(to Eliza, horrified)* You surely dont believe that your aunt was killed?

LIZA: Do I not! Them she lived with would have killed her for a hat-pin, let alone a hat.

MRS EYNSFORD HILL: But it cant have been right for your father to pour spirits down her throat like that. It might have killed her.

LIZA: Not her. Gin was mother's milk to her. . . .

And Liza, growing more and more at ease, launches into an account of the redemptive qualities of liquor in family life. She cannot be allowed to go on for too long, for the sake of both Mrs Higgins's 'at home' and the success of the scene, and so Higgins drops the hint: the experiment is over, Liza must now leave. Gracious 'Goodbyes' to Mrs Higgins and Colonel Pickering, a gracious 'Goodbye, all' to the others, then the too well-known conclusion:

> FREDDY: *(opening the door for her)* Are you walking across the Park, Miss Doolittle? If so—
>
> LIZA: *(with perfectly elegant diction)* Walk! Not bloody likely. *(Sensation)* I am going in a taxi.

With which final, shattering expletive Liza sails out. We must admit that modern faecal-minded drama and the familiarity of the scene to us all has reduced the sensational effect considerably; but it is no damp squib. It can never be, considering the purpose it serves over and above its aim to be shock-provoking.

The point at issue is whether to walk or take a taxi. Taxis, we may remember, had implied a good deal in Act I. To Freddy and his family they had meant simple necessities of existence, without which it became impossible to move; to Liza they had represented the height of luxury, mysteriously associated with Royalty and other symbols of the material ultimate. Now we have Freddy asking her to *walk* across the Park: for him it will mean a pleasant change, but for Liza it will somehow mean a return to the weariness and drudgery of her former life. So she rejects the invitation with all the emphasis and vigour her education in the gutters can muster for her. Her exit line is not simply a lurid piece of theatricality. It is an assertion of the awakening Life Force [Shaw's theory that mankind is continually improving]. It is, in the light of her background, inevitable and peculiarly right. By contrast, how pallid and sluttish the expression sounds when silly, superficial Clara uses it a few minutes later.

This, then, is the climax of a scene which since its auspicious opening has brilliantly balanced laughter against great seriousness of purpose. Liza is, of course, nothing more nor less than a doll, a triumph of artifice. She is a princess or a Cinderella doll at the moment of collision with her former existence. Beautifully intoned, phonetically perfect (if idiomatically unsound) words clothe grim suspicion, covetousness, and jealousy; they hang from the gaunt shoulders of ignorance and drunkenness and disease; they are the shimmering drapes round squalor and brutality and the sheer beastliness of poverty. They—these golden sounds of the phonetician's art—are the grotesques and Liza's squalid tale the truth.

The Eynsford Hill children are vastly entertained, and stand exposed. Deceived by appearances, they hear the comedy of the stricken aunt and drunken father as 'small talk', to be gleefully received and emulated. 'And it's so quaint, and gives such a smart emphasis to things that are not in themselves very witty', Clara says later. She could not damn herself more effectively.

A DEEPER MEANING

But Shaw exposes Liza as well, and we join Freddy in laughing at her. We should not be sentimentally evasive about this: Liza is an unmitigated incongruity in Mrs Higgins's drawing-room. The more she reveals of her incongruity the more we shall laugh at her—if we have a drawing-room point of view, if we have a middle-class point of view. . . .

But we should not imagine that this scene indulges us in the sort of humour which in [Shaw's play] *John Bull's Other Island* Shaw had forthrightly condemned. To have done so would have been a simple matter—and cruel; would have been merely to have Eliza go on uttering inanities like her weather report, thereby keeping her at a disadvantage throughout. The very opposite happens, the point of view shifts away from the drawing-room, the ethic turns upside down, and as Liza proceeds, it is as though the degradation and viciousness of the poor have gained the ascendancy. Nor—to the likes of the Doolittles of this world—is there anything funny in this. All is quite simply just so, normal, inoffensive, 'proper' and 'right'. The properness and rightness of her disclosures are points of honour with Liza, which she is prepared to defend in any squabble. And yet, what sordid proprieties, what squalid rights: what a guttersnipe soul this Cinderella still possesses!

Everyone stands indicted: Mrs Eynsford Hill by her genteel alarm, Freddy and Clara by their amusement, we—the audience—by our laughter, Liza by her poverty: indicted before the high tribunal of fact and its concomitant, that of common humanity, the implicit ethic that burns within the particulars of Liza's discourse. That stricken aunt, that drunken father, that hat, that hat-pin—these are all very, very amusing, yes. But these are images pointing to the

chasm between money and no money; education and ignorance; privilege and deprivation: the bedrock of our laughter, we are brought to realise, is a social and human tragedy.
Shaw's satire lies deep and may indeed be engulfed by
laughter—but when it is perceived it is disconcertingly
sharp. Comedy cannot be more masterfully realised.

Shaw's Social Experiments in *Pygmalion*

Michael Holroyd

Believing that the pen truly could be mightier than the sword and that language could have more effect on contemporary events than warfare, Shaw set out to conduct two social experiments in *Pygmalion*, according to biographer Michael Holroyd. Eliza is treated much as Dr. Frankenstein treats his monster, with complete scientific insensitivity. The subject of the second experiment, Eliza's father Alfred Doolittle, is an everyman figure. As Doolittle becomes a gentleman after receiving an income, Shaw suggests that moral reform depends on a reformed English economic system. Michael Holroyd's biographies include studies of painter Augustus John, writer Lytton Strachey, and a three-volume work about Bernard Shaw. He has also written a memoir, *Basil Street Blues*. He is married to the renowned English novelist Margaret Drabble.

[Shaw] enjoyed describing *Pygmalion* as an experiment to demonstrate how the science of phonetics could pull apart an antiquated British class system. 'The reformer we need most today is an energetic phonetic enthusiast,' he was to write in his Preface. This was Shaw's gesture towards removing the power for change from fighting men who were threatening to alter the world by warfare, and handing it to men of words whom he promoted as 'among the most important people in England at present.' In this context, the character of Henry Higgins (who appears as a comic version of Sherlock Holmes in Act I) takes his life from the revolutionary phonetician and philologist Henry Sweet, who had died while the play was being written. Writing to [English poet] Robert Bridges in 1910 about the need for a phonetic institute, he had described Sweet as the man 'I had most hopes of'. It was Bridges who, the following year, retained Shaw to speak at the Phonetic Conference on spelling reform at University College, London. 'It is perfectly easy to find a speaker whose speech will be accepted in every part of the English speaking world as valid 18-carat oral currency,' he wrote to Sweet afterwards, 'NOT that the pronunciation represented is the standard pronunciation or ideal pronunciation, or correct pronunciation, or in any way binding on any human being or morally superior to Hackney cockney [English dialectical speech] or Idaho american, but solely that if a man pronounces in that way he will be eligible as far as speech is concerned for the post of Lord Chief Justice, Chancellor at Oxford, Archbishop of Canterbury, Emperor, President, or Toast Master at the Mansion House.'

Two Experiments

It was this experiment that Shaw transferred to Higgins's laboratory in Wimpole Street, with its phonograph, laryngoscope, tuning-forks and organ pipes. This is a live experiment we are shown on stage, and as with all such laboratory work it is necessary for the Frankenstein doctor to behave as if his creation were insentient. 'She's incapable of understanding anything,' Higgins assures his fellow-scientist Colonel Pickering. 'Besides, do any of us understand what we are doing? If we did, would we ever do it?' When Pickering asks: 'Does it occur to you, Higgins, that the girl has some feelings?', Higgins cheerily replies: 'Oh no, I dont think so. Not any feelings that we need bother about. Have you, Eliza?'

Shaw conducts a second social experiment through Eliza's father, Alfred Doolittle, an elderly dustman of Dickensian vitality. Doolittle is any one of us. When asked by Higgins whether he is an honest man or rogue, he answers: 'A little of both, Henry, like the rest of us.' Being his name, he does as little as possible—some bribery here or there, a little blackmail, more drinking, an occasional change of mistress: and he provides positively no education at all for his illegitimate daughter 'except to give her a lick of the strap now and again'. Yet he has the quick wits and superficial charm of the capitalist entrepreneur. He is society's free man—free of responsibilities and conscience. 'Have you no morals, man?' demands Pickering. 'Cant afford them, Governor,' Doolittle answers. Undeserving poverty is his line: 'and I mean to go on being undeserving. I like it,' he adds. His disquisition on middle-class morality is intended by Shaw to have the same subversive effect as [Shakespeare's comic figure] Falstaff's discourse on honour.

Yet this is the man whom Shaw chooses as the first recipient of what he calculates to be a reasonable income-for-all. As the result of Higgins's joking reference to Doolittle as the most original moralist in England in a letter to an American philanthropist, the undeserving dustman is left £3,000. In Act II he had made his entrance with 'a professional flavour of dust about him'. In Act V when his name is announced and Pickering queries, 'Do you mean the dustman?', the parlourmaid answers: 'Dustman! Oh no, sir: a gentleman.' He is splendidly dressed as if for a fashionable wedding. Shaw's point is not that a gentleman is merely a dustman with money in the same way as a flower girl with phonetic training can be passed off as a duchess: it is that moral reformation depends upon the reform of our economic system. As Eric Bentley writes: 'He was giving the idea of the gentleman an economic basis.' It is this that Doolittle dreaded and derided, and now finds himself dragged into. 'It's making a gentleman of me that I object to,' he protests. '. . . I have to live for others and not for myself: thats middle class morality.'

THE RELATIONSHIP OF HIGGINS AND ELIZA

Under Higgins's tutelage Eliza becomes a doll of 'remarkable distinction . . . speaking with pedantic correctness of pronunciation and great beauty of tone', which Mrs. Higgins tells her son is 'a triumph of your art and of her dressmaker's'. This dummy figure replaces the 'draggle tailed guttersnipe' whose life Higgins acknowledges to have been real, warm and violent. The classical Pygmalion had prayed to [Greek goddess] Aphrodite to make his ideal statue come alive so that he could marry her. Shaw's flower girl, whom Higgins has manufactured into a replica duchess by the beginning of Act IV, is transformed into an independent woman whom Higgins refuses to marry. However, the transformation scene, in which Higgins lays his hands on Eliza like a sculptor's creative act, is a struggle the implications of which are sexual:

'Eliza tries to control herself . . . she is on the point of screaming
. . . He comes to her . . . He pulls her up . . . Liza [breathless] . . .

She crisps her fingers frantically. HIGGINS *[looking at her in cool wonder]* . . . LIZA *[gives a suffocated scream of fury, and instinctively darts her nails at his face]!!* HIGGINS *[catching her wrists . . . He throws her roughly into the easy chair]* LIZA *[crushed by superior strength and weight].* HIGGINS *[thundering]* Those slippers LIZA *[with bitter submission]* Those slippers'

These stage directions contain many sado-masochistic undertones. But Higgins himself resists every innuendo. This was important to Shaw. For, remembering Sweet's genius for 'making everything impossible', he turned his mind to another 'genius' as a model for Higgins, the author of *The Voice*, Vandeleur Lee. Higgins's asexual association with Eliza is consequently authorized by Shaw's faith in his mother's 'innocence', and written as an endorsement of his own legitimacy. The platonic arrangement depends on the professional circumstances of their relationship. 'You see, she'll be a pupil,' Higgins explains to Pickering, 'and teaching would be impossible unless pupils were sacred.' Higgins's voice tuition of Eliza takes the place of the singing lessons Lee had given [Shaw's mother] Bessie (Lucinda Elizabeth Shaw) and to reinforce this substitution Shaw provides Higgins's pupil with the same name as Lee's pupil:

HIGGINS Whats your name?

THE FLOWER GIRL Liza Doolittle

HIGGINS *[declaiming gravely]* Eliza, Elizabeth, Betsy and Bess, They went to the wood to get a bird's nes'.

'I've never been able to feel really grown-up and tremendous, like other chaps,' Higgins tells Pickering. He explains the reason to his mother who has regretted his inability to fall in love with any woman under forty-five. 'My idea of a lovable woman is somebody as like you as possible,' he tells her. 'I shall never get into the way of seriously liking young women: some habits lie too deep to be changed.'

In his final act, Shaw was rewriting the legend of Svengali [the evil hypnotist in the novel by George du Maurier] and his pupil Trilby. When Svengali dies of a heart attack, Trilby's voice is silenced, she cannot sing at her concert, and she follows Svengali into death. In Shaw's version Eliza's true voice is heard once she emerges from Higgins's bullying presence and walks out to a separate life. But other forces were at work in the final act obliging Higgins himself to speak increasingly with the voice of G.B.S. [George Bernard Shaw], the public figure that had developed from

Vandeleur Lee; while Eliza comes to represent the emotions that [actress] Stella Campbell was introducing into his life. Higgins's description of Eliza as a 'consort battleship' has something of the armoured impregnability Shaw attributed to his mother ('one of those women who could act as matron of a cavalry barracks from eighteen to forty and emerge without a stain on her character'). But no one else in the play regards Eliza in this light. Mrs. Higgins calls her 'naturally rather affectionate'; Doolittle admits she is 'very tender-hearted'; and Eliza herself demands: 'Every girl has a right to be loved.'

What Higgins wants is less clear. He claims he has created an ideal wife—'a consort for a king'—yet he must resist her emotional appeal: 'I wont stop for you . . . I can do without anybody.' The purpose of Higgins's experiment has been 'filling up the deepest gulf that separates class from class and soul from soul'. It is half successful, half a failure. The class gulf is filled at the garden party, dinner party and reception: the gulf between Eliza and Higgins remains. Eliza has changed, but Higgins admits 'I cant change my nature.' He seems 'cold, unfeeling, selfish' to Eliza. 'I only want to be natural,' she says. But can Higgins be natural? Where will things lead if she accepts his invitation to go back to him 'for the fun of it'?

THE AMBIGUOUS ENDING

The original ending of the play is carefully ambiguous, reflecting Shaw's uncertainties over his romance with Stella. He could not marry her: she could not remain for ever his pupil as an actress learning from his theatrical direction. But might they become lovers? The question is left open to our imagination:

> MRS. HIGGINS I'm afraid youve spoilt that girl, Henry. But never mind, dear: I'll buy you the tie and gloves.
>
> HIGGINS [*sunnily*] Oh, dont bother. She'll buy em all right enough. Good-bye. *They kiss. Mrs. Higgins runs out. Higgins, left alone, rattles his cash in his pocket; chuckles; and disports himself in a highly self-satisfied manner.*

This, as Eric Bentley argues, 'is the true naturalistic [after naturalism, the theory that a human is only a higher order of animal] ending'. But Shaw's subsequent attempts to clear up its ambiguity have blurred the outline of its elegant structure. The faint poignancy of the ending lies in the half-emergent realization that there is to be no satisfactory marriage for this Cinderella; while a feminist reading tells us that Higgins cannot be approved of as a husband. But the public wanted the Miltonic bachelor to be transformed into the beautiful lady's husband. 'This is unbearable,' Shaw cried out. Once his love affair with Stella had ended, he could not bear to speculate on what might have happened when 'I almost condescended to romance'. 'Eliza married Freddy [Eynsford-Hill],' he [wrote]; 'and the notion of her marrying Higgins is disgusting.' In other words Eliza married a double-barrelled nonentity like George Cornwallis-West [whom Stella married], and Higgins's agonizing boredom with the Eynsford-Hill family reflects Shaw's own impatience with the smart visitors who sometimes crowded him out of Stella's house.

The history of *Pygmalion* was to develop into a struggle over this ending. For the play's first publication in book form in 1916, Shaw added a sequel recounting 'what Eliza did'. Her decision not to marry Higgins, he explained, was well-considered. The differences between them of age and income, when added to Higgins's mother-fixation and exclusive passion for phonetics, was too wide a gulf to bridge. He told the story of Eliza and Freddy, Mr. and Mrs. Eynsford-Hill, as invitingly as he could: but the public went on preferring its own version. Shaw made his final version of the end on 19 August 1939:

> MRS. HIGGINS I'm afraid youve spoilt that girl, Henry. I should be uneasy about you and her if she were less fond of Colonel Pickering.
>
> HIGGINS Pickering! Nonsense: she's going to marry Freddy. Ha ha! Freddy! Freddy!! Ha ha ha ha ha!!!!! [*He roars with laughter as the play ends*]

But by now this laughter sounded as hollow as Higgins's prediction, and even Shaw's printers had begun to query his intentions.

Socialist Themes in *Pygmalion*

Arthur Ganz

George Bernard Shaw's socialist concerns are not immediately evident in *Pygmalion*. However, Arthur Ganz purports that Shaw's study of a poor woman's rise, coupled with her father's movement into middle-class respectability, incorporates ideas Shaw held as a member of the Fabian Society, a socialist group. The Fabians believed in the eventual evolution of mankind into a classless society, and Eliza's rise suggests that such societal mobility is possible through education and intermarriage. Doolittle's rise is a serious parody of Eliza's and mocks conventional romantic notions that the mere acquisition of money and social prestige will lead to a happy ending. Arthur Ganz has taught at the City University of New York. His books include *Realms of the Self: Variations on a Theme in Modern Drama, Literary Terms,* and *George Bernard Shaw,* from which this excerpt is taken.

Pygmalion does not at first glance seem like a socialist, much less a Fabian play, but it is. Higgins, who appears to notice little beyond his professional concerns, has noticed— no doubt in deference to the social interests of his author— with regard to flower girls and their like that 'a woman of that class looks like a worn out drudge of fifty a year after she's married'. Later Higgins explains to his mother that changing Eliza into a different being by 'creating a new speech for her' is 'filling up the deepest gulf that separates class from class and soul from soul'. These remarks, and especially the latter, cast a suggestive light on Act I, which is more than a charmingly imaginative prologue to the story of the 'squashed cabbage leaf' passed off as 'the Queen of

Excerpted from *George Bernard Shaw,* by Arthur Ganz (London: Macmillan, 1983). Copyright © Arthur Ganz, 1983. Reprinted by permission of Palgrave.

Sheba'; it is a survey of the social, as well as linguistic distance Eliza must traverse from 'the gutter' with its 'kerbstone English' to the lower classes with their shrewd recognitions of marks of distinctions ('e's a genleman: look at his ba-oots') and latent hostility to the gentry ('You take us for dirt under your feet, dont you?'), to the shabby genteel (Shaw's own class) represented by the Eynsford-Hills, to the comfortable assurance of money and position embodied in Pickering. It is reasonable to suppose that the elimination of such nefarious social distinctions and the gradual—that is, Fabian—evolution of a classless society in which speech patterns are not a barrier is the ultimate aim of Higgins's Universal Alphabet, at least in Shaw's view (after all, the creation of a similar alphabet was the cause to which Shaw left his substantial estate). But the matter, being Shavian, does not end there. Egalitarianism is desirable not only to achieve social justice but for an even higher purpose: so that all shall be intermarriageable, that is, so that the Life Force [a vital force that causes evolution in nature] can select couples from the total gene-pool of the population and thus have the widest latitude in breeding the Superman.

This consideration returns us again to the play's romantic, or in the full Shavian sense, sexual concerns. Eliza's demands, after she has by Higgins' efforts and her will been raised to a higher level of being, may have a metaphorical aspect, but that does not make them any less urgent. And from the point of view of the Life Force, Higgins would seem to be more suitable breeding material than Freddy. However, Higgins is not only a prospective father for Eliza's children, as her 'creator', he stands to some extent in a paternal relation to her already. Since Doolittle is her biological progenitor, Eliza has two fathers in the play, neither of whom, Shaw claims at the end of the Postscript, she likes. In actuality, Eliza addresses her father cosily as 'dad' in the last act and seems quaintly snobbish and jealous of his marrying her stepmother, 'that low common woman'. Nevertheless, she is glad enough to see the last of him in Act II, for she understands that he has come only to get money out of her new protectors and does not seem to understand, or sympathise with, his originality of character.

Since he has come to sell her for five pounds we pardon Eliza's insensitivity on this point even as we delight in the ingenuity with which Doolittle, one of Shaw's supreme comic creations, manipulates bourgeois sentimentality ('a father's heart, as it were') while seeing through the hypocrisies of 'middle-class morality', as in this . . . exchange with Pickering, who is shocked at Doolittle's view of his daughter as a commercial property:

> PICKERING: Have you no morals, man?
>
> DOOLITTLE: [*unabashed*] Cant afford them, Governor. Neither could you if you was as poor as me.

(Doolittle should not be granted too much charm, however; compare the amiability of Stanley Holloway's performance as perpetuated in the film of *My Fair Lady* with the extra acerbity of Wilfred Lawson's characterisation, hinting at genuine coarseness and brutality, in the [Gabriel] Pascal film of the play.) But despite his lack of 'morals' and his characterisation of himself as 'one of the undeserving poor', Doolittle seems cheerfully committed to the work ethic, assuring Higgins that he will spend the five pounds on a spree and will not 'live idle' on it (idleness, we recall, is Shaw's bête noire [pet peeve]): 'I'll have to go to work same as if I'd never had it. It wont pauperize me, you bet'.

Perhaps it is this latent respectability, as well as his fear of the workhouse . . . that makes him vulnerable to the bequest that Higgins partially thrusts upon him. For just as Higgins raises Eliza from the gutter to win a bet, so he elevates her father to make a joke. Not only are the actions parallel but they are neither of them motivated by a personal concern for the recipient. In both cases the results of this 'godlike' intervention are difficult to assess. Doolittle is saved from the workhouse, but he has lost his capacity for self-gratification, his 'happiness' as he repeatedly says. . . .

Moreover he must now marry his 'missus', who—in a delicious comic reversal of conventional romantic suppositions—has, he tells us, 'been very low, thinking of the happy days that are no more'. For the climax of Doolittle's story, as he goes off resplendently dressed to be married at St George's Hanover Square, is what many audiences have hoped would be the climax of his daughter's. Quite in the manner of an Elizabethan dramatist, Shaw makes the subplot of *Pygmalion* a darkly comic parody of the romantic element latent in the main plot.

Shaw's Problem with the English Language

Ruth Adam

In this selection, Ruth Adam discusses George
Bernard Shaw's contention that much was wrong
with the English language. In particular, there were
not enough vowels to suggest adequately how words
were really pronounced. Because so many English
people spoke the language in so many different
ways, pronunciation became an indicator of social
class, and Shaw set out in *Pygmalion* to expose this
problem. Shaw proposed a new English alphabet
with at least forty letters, and he even left money in
his will to enact his plan. Ruth Adam worked as a
teacher in England before going on to write a dozen
novels, including *I'm Not Complaining*. She has also
written a textbook on American history and a history
of feminism in the twentieth century.

Shaw said "The English have no respect for their language
and will not teach their children to speak it. . . . It is impossible for an Englishman to open his mouth without making
some other Englishman despise him."

This is part of the class-consciousness perpetuated by the
British education system, in which you acquire an accent
which will identify you by class for ever after. But it works
both ways. The Etonian [one who attends the English College Eton] learns to despise those without an Etonian accent.
But the working man who despises gentlemanly parasites
guards against being confused with them. In [Shaw's play]
Man and Superman, the hero always introduces his chauf-
feur as "Mr Enry Straker" because, "This man takes more
trouble to drop his aitches than ever his father did to pick
them up. It's a mark of caste to him. I have never met anybody more swollen with the pride of class than Enry is."

THE PROBLEM WITH THE ENGLISH LANGUAGE

The reason for the difference of accents in the first place is because the English alphabet has not enough vowels in it to express the different sounds of the language. Even when you use combinations of vowels there is no general agreement about the pronunciation, and not all of the consonants have any agreed speech value. Therefore it is impossible to teach yourself what the language should sound like from reading it, and so the speech of the English is slipshod, ugly and incomprehensible. Shaw wrote *Pygmalion* to illustrate his argument that we need a phonetic alphabet. It delighted him that a subject which sounded so dry and didactic should turn out to be the most popular of all his plays. In the play, Professor Higgins, a phonetics expert, transforms a Cockney flower-girl into a society lady by teaching her to speak beautifully.

HIGGINS. A woman who utters such depressing and disgusting sounds has no right to be anywhere—no right to live. Remember that you are a human being with a soul and the divine gift of articulate speech: that your native language is the language of Shakespeare and Milton and the Bible: and dont sit there crooning like a bilious pigeon.

ELIZA (*quite overwhelmed, looking up at him in mingled wonder and deprecation without daring to raise her head*). Ah-ah-ah-ow-ow-ow-oo!

HIGGINS (*whipping out his book*). Heavens! What a sound! (*He writes, then holds out the book and reads, reproducing her vowels exactly*). Ah-ah-ah ow ow-ow-oo!

ELIZA (*tickled by the performance and laughing in spite of herself*). Garn!

HIGGINS. You see this creature with her kerbstone English: the English that will keep her in the gutter to the end of her days. Well, sir, in three months I could pass that girl off as a duchess at an ambassador's garden party. I could even get her a place as a lady's maid or shop assistant which requires better English.

A SCANDALOUS WORD

Shaw's most-quoted line of all occurs in this play, at the point where Eliza is half-way through her re-education. She can now articulate perfectly and pronounce every word correctly. But her language and the content of her conversation still belong to her East-End background. Higgins tries her out by sending her to make a formal call in a Kensington drawing-room. She manages to talk and behave well enough to pass as a lady until the last moment, when an infatuated young man is seeing her out.

> FREDDY (*opening the door for her*). Are you walking across the Park, Miss Doolittle? If so—
>
> ELIZA (*with perfectly elegant diction*). Walk? Not bloody likely. (*Sensation*). I am going in a taxi.

In 1913, this line caused a tremendous furore. Audiences were delightedly shocked, and the press wrote about it for a whole week. Shaw said afterwards that although he had been writing seriously about the coming war and how it could be avoided, for years before, no one had taken any notice, but that this one word made him instantly famous, beyond the Kaiser [German leader], the Tsar [Russian leader], Shakespeare and [Greek poet] Homer and President [Woodrow] Wilson. By the time *Pygmalion* became *My Fair Lady* "bloody" had become allowable. It was regarded as only slightly blasphemous slang among educated and uneducated people alike, either because the social climate had become less strict, or because Shaw's line had become a catch-phrase and so familiar. The script-writers of the musical version thought it no longer carried the joke it was meant to, and substituted a line in which Eliza refers to a "ruddy arse". But (like most rewritten jokes) it missed the mark.

SHAW'S ECCENTRIC SPELLING

In his earlier plays, when Shaw wanted to convey the particular pronunciation of any character, he spelt the words out phonetically, a habit which makes parts of the plays tiresome to read. An American is always presented as saying "dullicate" for delicate. In *John Bull's Other Island* he conveys an Irish brogue by writing out "dhat" for that, "Prodestan" for Protestant, "hwat" for what and so on. In *Major Barbara* he wants to reproduce Cockney speech: " Wot prawce selvytion nah?" But it took him a long time, and Shaw was impatient. He had begun his career as a public speaker and always found writing slow after it. He thought, as he said, in dialogue, and so his thought outran the speed of his pen. Because of this he learned shorthand and kept it up so that even after ninety he could still compose fifteen hundred words a day.

He had some private foibles of his own about the appearance of his printed work. He refused to use the apostrophe in such colloquial phrases as "can't" and "don't", writing them as "cant" and "dont" instead. He disliked commas. He said that the Bible would never have attained its supreme position in literature if it had been disfigured with such unsightly signs.

A NEW ALPHABET

After he had met Henry Sweet, an eccentric phonetics expert from Oxford—and the original of Professor Higgins in the play—Shaw began to work out the idea of a new British alphabet which would transform the language and save time in writing it. The Proposed British Alphabet was to have at least forty letters. Even so, said Shaw, it would not pretend to be exhaustive. "It contains only sixteen vowels whereas by infinitesimal movements of the tongue countless different vowels can be produced, all of them in use among speakers of English who utter the same vowels no oftener than they

---

GEORGE BERNARD SHAW ON THE ENGLISH AND THEIR LANGUAGE

In this excerpt, Shaw sounds off on the inability of the English to speak their language correctly.

The English have no respect for their language, and will not teach their children to speak it. They spell it so abominably that no man can teach himself what it sounds like. It is impossible for an Englishman to open his mouth without making some other Englishman hate or despise him. German and Spanish are accessible to foreigners: English is not accessible even to Englishmen. The reformer England needs today is an energetic phonetic enthusiast: that is why I have made such a one the hero of a popular play. There have been heroes of that kind crying in the wilderness for many years past. . . .

Pygmalion has been an extremely successful play all over Europe and North America as well as at home. It is so intensely and deliberately didactic, and its subject is esteemed so dry, that I delight in throwing it at the heads of the wiseacres who repeat the parrot cry that art should never be didactic. It goes to prove my contention that art should never be anything else.

George Bernard Shaw, *Shaw: An Autobiography, 1898–1950: The Playwright Years.* Ed. Stanley Weintraub. New York: Weybright and Talley, 1970.

make the same fingerprints. Nevertheless they can understand one another's speech and writing sufficiently to converse and correspond: for instance, a graduate of Trinity College Dublin has no difficulty in understanding a graduate of Oxford university when one says that 'the sun rohze' and the other that 'the sun raheoze' nor are either of them puzzled when a peasant calls his childhood his 'chawldid'. For a university graduate calls my native country 'Awlind.'" Shaw suggested that the letter "O" should have different vowel-signs for its various pronunciations in "on", "oak", "out", "wool" and "ooze". Consonants should be rationalized, with different signs for "th" as in "thigh", "they", and different signs again for "su" according to whether it was pronounced as in "measure" or in "sure".

In his old age Shaw became more and more interested in the idea of the foundation of a new alphabet and left a part of his money to establish a fund to get it launched. He directed his trustees to arrange for research and reports and for a model set of signs to be drawn up. As a basic pronunciation, they were to take "that recorded of His Majesty our late King George V and sometimes described as Northern English". When the form of the alphabet had been finally agreed upon Shaw ordered that an expert was then to translate [his play] *Androcles and the Lion* into it, and that the play was to be published with the ordinary version and on each opposite page its facsimile in the Proposed British Alphabet. These instructions of Shaw's have now been carried out and you can find the *Shaw Alphabet Edition of Androcles and the Lion* in any public library, looking like this:

ᴧᒐᒐᴄᴄᴎ?. ᴣˊᴦ ᴎᴎ ᴧ ᴦᴆᴎᴉᴤᴉ, ᴉᴎ: ᴣ ᴊᴦ ᴦ ᴆᴉᴤᴎᴎᴎ.

ᴧᴖᴣᴆᴦ. ᴧᴄ, ᴉᴎᴎ ᴩᴎᴎ ᴩ ᴤᴦᴦ ᴆᴉᴎ, ᴏᴎᴄᴎ ᴎᴎ ᴎᴣᴎ ᴎᴖᴤ?

Shaw's Implicit Subjugation of Women in *Pygmalion*

J. Ellen Gainor

This feminist reading of *Pygmalion* makes a number of provocative assertions. J. Ellen Gainor claims that in addition to its similarities to the Pygmalion and Cinderella stories, Shaw's play resembles Snow White, with Henry Higgins playing the role of the evil stepmother. *Pygmalion* dramatizes the subjection of Eliza Doolittle and implicitly suggests that women can never be appropriate teachers. Gainor compares Mrs. Pearce's cleansing of Eliza to rape, and scenes from the original film of *Pygmalion* supply additional evidence for this suggestion. Eliza's final break from Higgins seems at first to be a "refreshingly feminist twist," until we learn in the "sequel" that she is financially and emotionally dependent on Pickering and Higgins, respectively, for years to come. J. Ellen Gainor has taught at Cornell University. She is the coeditor of *Performing America: Cultural Nationalism in American Theater* and *Imperialism and Theatre: Essays on World Theatre, Drama, and Performance* and the author of *Shaw's Daughters: Dramatic and Narrative Constructions of Gender*, from which this essay is excerpted.

It is intriguing that Shaw conflates two seemingly separate myths in the play, the Pygmalion story and a fairy-tale plot that overtly resembles *Cinderella* in its transformation of ragged young woman to "princess," but also more subtly invokes *Snow White*. The French feminist critic Hélène Cixous shows the connection between these male-authored myths— a connection that fits the Shavian rendition peculiarly well.

One cannot yet say of the following history "it's just a story."
It's a tale still true today. Most women who have awakened
remember having slept, *having been put to sleep.*

Once upon a time . . . once . . . and once again.

Beauties slept in their woods, waiting for princes to come and
wake them up. In their beds, in their glass coffins, in their
childhood forests like dead women. Beautiful, but passive;
hence desirable: all mystery emanates from them. It is men
who like to play dolls. As we have known since Pygmalion.
Their old dream: to be god the mother. The best mother, the
second mother, the one who gives the second birth.

Through Mrs. Higgins's censure of Pickering and her son,
Shaw expresses his understanding, parallel to Cixous's
analysis, of the "artist-men": "You certainly are a pretty pair
of babies, playing with your live doll." Shaw's fairy-tale allu-
sions make the connection even more apt. Shaw also includes strategic references to the Snow White tale, which features in many versions the famous glass coffin, and, more
important, the queen's magic mirror and her poisoned apple.

ELIZA AND SNOW WHITE

In the well-known Grimm version of the tale, the evil queen,
stepmother to Snow White, disguises herself as an old ped-
dler to seek out the young princess, who is hiding from her
in the forest at the home of the dwarfs. She brings with her
an apple, half of which has been poisoned. She tricks Snow
White into sharing the apple with her, by breaking it in two
and safely eating the unadulterated portion. The poisoned
bite that Snow White takes becomes lodged in her throat as
she falls into a deathlike sleep. In *Pygmalion,* Shaw casts
Higgins in the stepmother role, as he tries to seduce Eliza
into staying to learn to talk like a duchess:

> HIGGINS (*snatching a chocolate cream from the piano, his eyes
> suddenly beginning to twinkle with mischief*) Have some
> chocolates, Eliza.
>
> LIZA (*halting, tempted*) How do I know what might be in
> them? Ive heard of girls being drugged by the like of you. (*Hig-
> gins whips out his penknife; cuts a chocolate in two; puts one
> half into his mouth and bolts it; and offers her the other half.*)
>
> HIGGINS. Pledge of good faith, Eliza. I eat one half: you eat the
> other. (*Liza opens her mouth to retort: he pops the half choco-
> late into it*). You shall have boxes of them, every day. You shall
> live on them. Eh?
>
> LIZA (*who has disposed of the chocolate after being nearly*

choked by it) I wouldnt have ate it, only I'm too ladylike to take it out of my mouth.

Eliza's room in Higgins's house also contains a full-length mirror, the first one she has ever encountered. In the Snow White tale, the stepmother learns from the magic mirror of Snow White's whereabouts as well as of her own loss of superior beauty. Although Shaw does not use this prop as exactly, he does imbue it with the evil connotations of the fairy-tale (from Eliza's viewpoint), and it does become a vehicle for self-appraisal and self-recognition. After Eliza's bath in act 2, she sees an unrecognizable self in the mirror for the first time. Reflecting her puritanical upbringing, she feels the vision of her naked body is indecent, and she covers it with a towel. Yet it also reveals her physical beauty, and thus the mirror "tells" the same news as in the fairy-tale. The mirror reappears in the last scene of act 4, moreover, to demonstrate Eliza's disenchantment with the image of herself created by Higgins. Dressed in the clothes Pickering has provided, surrounded by the furnishings Higgins has procured, Eliza rejects her reflection as she severs the tie with Wimpole Street, sticking her tongue out at the mirror princess who has achieved Higgins's ideal as she exits her room for the last time, leaving fairy land behind.

HENRY AS EVIL STEPMOTHER

Shaw's association of Higgins with the evil stepmother adds a dark tone to *Pygmalion*—one that contrasts with the fairy godmother transformation of the slavey Cinderella. This shading in the play finds its strongest evidence in the repeated threats to Eliza's sexual and physical safety. Critic Martin Meisel centers this action in "the seduction scene of the second act," where "everyone suspects Higgins' designs." But the theme is introduced much earlier, in the opening scene of the play, with her first "terrified" and "hysterical" insistence of her respectability and the fear of losing her "character." Eliza's concerns operate on two levels here: not only does she fear a loss of reputation (meaning actually the acquisition of one as a loose woman) and legal livelihood, but her speech also foreshadows the larger issue of Eliza's loss of self—the transformation into a new identity and "character" created by Higgins.

From her act 1 protestation that "I'm a good girl, I am" through her act 5 taunt to Henry, "Wring away. What do I care? I knew youd strike me some day," Eliza consistently expresses concern for her physical and moral well-being at the hands of her teacher and surrogate father Higgins. Both Higgins and the bystanders at Covent Garden identify the former with teaching, and Shaw establishes the didactic nature of the drama in its brief preface. But he explicitly fuses paternal and pedagogical roles with the threat of physical violence early in act 2:

> MRS. PEARCE. Dont cry, you silly girl. Sit down. Nobody is going to touch your money.

> HIGGINS. Somebody is going to touch you, with a broomstick, if you dont stop snivelling. Sit down.

> LIZA (*obeying slowly*) Ah-ah-ah-ow-oo-o! One would think you was my father.

> HIGGINS. If I decide to teach you, I'll be worse than two fathers to you.

Higgins, of course, is actually one of three fathers for Eliza, the other two being Colonel Pickering—another teacher from whom she "learnt really nice manners"—and "the regulation natural chap," Alfred Doolittle. These three men represent the social spectrum of patriarchy, each with his own mode of keeping Eliza "in her place." Doolittle, who knows nothing of the didactic arrangement under which Eliza will stay at Wimpole Street, arrives at the house to arrange the "sale" of his daughter for five pounds, acting out the exchange of women in patriarchal culture. He makes the Victorian assumption that Higgins's job, as the prospective husband in this burlesqued exchange, will be to "improve Eliza's mind" and suggests that the most efficacious method will be "with a strap."

ISSUES OF SEX AND CLASS

Unbeknownst to Doolittle, of course, Higgins manipulates their conversation so that the member of "the undeserving poor" will reveal his class differences and prejudices. Eliza, from the same class origins, is a victim of both class and sex discrimination, and Shaw draws parallels between these two forms of injustice in the play. Although Eliza repeatedly asserts her essential similarity to the upper classes, with whom she shares self-respect and human feelings, Higgins maintains a stance in opposition to her beliefs.

> PICKERING (*in good-humored remonstrance*) Does it occur to

you, Higgins, that the girl has some feelings?

HIGGINS (*looking critically at her*) Oh no, I dont think so. Not any feelings that we need bother about. (*Cheerily*) Have you, Eliza?

LIZA. I got my feelings same as anyone else.

Through Higgins's infantilization of Eliza, treating her as a child and talking about her as if she weren't present or able to understand, Shaw creates a parallel between issues of class and sex: discrimination toward the poor and toward women (who are tantamount to children) appear very similar. By erasing detectable class difference in Eliza through speech education, Higgins believes he will be endowing her with the humanity she lacks. The issue of Eliza's sex, however, does not enter into Higgins's equation in any considered way. Speech training and gender programming go hand in hand with Higgins's method, and thus as Eliza learns Henry's speech, she also absorbs the masculine context from which it evolved.

Late in the play, Henry delivers the first of his "creation" speeches, fulfilling his Pygmalion image: "I have created this thing out of the squashed cabbage leaves of Covent Garden." Eliza clarifies this creative, educational process, highlighting the masculine nature of his precepts: "I was brought up to be just like him, unable to control myself, and using bad language on the slightest provocation." In other words, Higgins has reared Eliza in his own image, a male image. Significantly, language, the instrument of male paternity, is the medium through which Eliza assumes her resemblance to Higgins. As Mrs. Higgins observes:

MRS. HIGGINS. You silly boy, of course she's not presentable. She's a triumph of your art and of her dress maker's; but if you suppose for a moment that she doesnt give herself away in every sentence she utters, you must be perfectly cracked about her.

PICKERING. But dont you think something might be done? I mean something to eliminate the sanguinary element from her conversation?

MRS. HIGGINS. Not as long as she is in Henry's hands.

HIGGINS (*aggrieved*) Do you mean that *my* language is improper?

MRS. HIGGINS. No, dearest: it would be quite proper—say on a canal barge; but it would not be proper for her at a garden party.

Mrs. Higgins opposes the masculine realm of the canal barge to the more feminine location, the garden party, and shows that Eliza speaks her teacher's masculine language. Eliza confirms this, speaking of both the class and sexual nature of language:

> You told me, you know, that when a child is brought to a foreign country, it picks up the language in a few weeks, and forgets its own. Well, I am a child in your country. I have forgotten my own language, and can speak nothing but yours. Thats the real break-off with the corner of Tottenham Court Road.

In act 4, after Eliza's triumph, when she expresses anger and frustration over the men's insensitivity to her dominant role in the success, Higgins remarks, "Youre not bad-looking: it's quite a pleasure to look at you sometimes—not now, of course, because youre crying and looking as ugly as the very devil; but when youre all right and quite yourself." The subtext of his comment, "when you behave in a feminine fashion—that is, crying or being temperamental—you are 'not yourself,' not the creature I made," comes through clearly. When in act 5 Eliza asserts her independence Higgins exclaims triumphantly—in the same manner in which Shaw's avuncular persona instructed "his" Dorothea—"By George, Eliza, I said I'd make a woman of you; and I have. I like you like this." Her attainment of Higgins's sense of "womanhood" allows her access to male identity: "Now youre a tower of strength: a consort battleship. You and I and Pickering will be three old bachelors instead of only two men and a silly girl."

CLARA EYNSFORD-HILL AND ELIZA

In shorter form, Shaw reinforces the paternal education of Eliza by creating a parallel scenario for Clara Eynsford-Hill in his "sequel," the prose epilogue that follows the play. Clara becomes Eliza's legal sister through the latter's marriage to her brother Freddy Eynsford-Hill, and spiritual sister through her education into moral, socially conscious humanity. Clara, "who appeared to Higgins and his mother as a disagreeable and ridiculous person, and to her own mother as in some inexplicable way a social failure, had never seen herself in either light," not, at least, until she read [English novelist] H.G. Wells and [English novelist John] Galsworthy. Clara, Shaw tells us, formed "a gushing desire to take her [Eliza] for a model," but experienced quite a shock

when she learned "that this exquisite apparition had gradu-
ated from the gutter in a few months time."

> It shook her so violently, that when Mr. H.G. Wells lifted her
> on the point of his puissant pen, and placed her at the angle
> of view from which the life she was leading and the society to
> which she clung appeared in its true relation to real human
> needs and worthy social structure, he effected a conversion
> and a conviction of sin comparable to the most sensational
> feats of General Booth.

Thus Clara, through male literary paternity, similarly
achieves a laudable social stature, having taken the authors'
precepts to heart and having substituted them as her models. In the process, of course, Clara leaves her mother's conventional views and her circle at Large-lady Park.

> It exasperated her to think that the dungeon in which she had
> languished for so many unhappy years had been unlocked all
> the time, and that the impulses she had so carefully struggled
> with and stifled for the sake of keeping well with society,
> were precisely those by which alone she could have come
> into any sort of sincere human contact.

Clara, another princess locked away, learns from Galsworthy of the potential that lay within her all the time. By negative association with her mother and her mother's circle,
these unspecified "impulses" take on masculine qualities.

FAILED MATRIARCHS

The maternal rejection presented in this sequel also continues a matriarchal theme from the main drama. Eliza is another of Shaw's orphan characters, having been brought up
in a motherless home: "I aint got no mother. Her that turned
me out was my sixth stepmother. But I done without them."
Higgins offers his housekeeper, Mrs. Pearce, as a maternal
substitute for the girl: "You can adopt her, Mrs. Pearce: I'm
sure a daughter would be a great amusement to you," and
indeed entrusts this older woman with all domestic matters
relating to Eliza's stay, including those feminine matters of
hygiene inappropriate for him to supervise. Shaw establishes Mrs. Pearce as a parallel character to Higgins's
mother, a domineering, scolding, condescending woman,
who is the object of Henry's continual rebellion. As such, the
mothers are both ineffectual teacher figures; their "boy"
Henry never carries out their instructions, particularly with
regard to his pupil, Eliza:

> Then might I ask you not to come down to breakfast in your

dressing-gown, or at any rate not to use it as a napkin to the extent you do, sir. And if you would be so good as not to eat everything off the same plate, and to remember not to put the porridge saucepan out of your hand on the clean tablecloth, it would be a better example to the girl. You know you nearly choked yourself with a fishbone in the jam only last week.

The women's failure as teachers corresponds to Higgins's patriarchal belief in pedagogy as a masculine occupation. This also accounts for his surprising reaction to Eliza's notion of being an elocution instructor. As the "assistant to that hairyfaced Hungarian," Eliza would place herself in the traditionally feminine position of inferiority, appropriating male privilege while maintaining a feminine identity. This prompts Higgins's threat to "wring your neck." But when Eliza realizes her ability to perform independently, to mirror her teacher/father instead of compete with him via feminine affiliation with another male, his response is altogether different. Eliza cries,

> Aha! Now I know how to deal with you. What a fool I was not to think of it before! You cant take away the knowledge you gave me. You said I had a finer ear than you. . . . I'll advertize it in the papers that your duchess is only a flower girl that you taught, and that she'll teach anybody to be a duchess just the same in six months for a thousand guineas.

Her discovery elicits his above-quoted exclamation of pleasure with the woman he has "made," a woman who to his eyes resembles a man like himself. This characterological mirroring corresponds to the physical mirror emblem that runs through the play. Higgins's mirror reflects Higgins in Eliza, a correlation he confirms at the end of act 4, after the passage quoted earlier about her not being "herself" when she, essentially, does not project his image of her. He tells her, "You go to bed and have a good nice rest; and then get up and look at yourself in the glass; and you wont feel so cheap."

THE "RAPE" OF ELIZA

The disparagement of Eliza, calling her "cheap" and a "dirty slut" again has class connotations, with a heavily sexual undertone. Mrs. Pearce echoes Higgins's defamation of Eliza, and as his minion she enters into the darker mythic subplot discussed earlier. Higgins informs Eliza in act 2, "If youre naughty and idle you will sleep in the back kitchen among the black beetles, and be walloped by Mrs. Pearce with a broomstick." Despite Higgins's numerous threats of physical violence, he never actually hurts Eliza, mental and emotional cruelty notwithstanding. Instead, Shaw projects onto Mrs. Pearce the physical, sexual violation of Eliza that Henry suppresses throughout, in a lesbian "rape" scene added to the original script at the time it was filmed.

Higgins insists that Mrs. Pearce "bundle her off to the bath-room" to clean her as a first step toward respectability. This action fits neatly with the mythic "rebirth" of Eliza, for bathing has always been symbolically associated with the remission of sin and rebirth in the Western Christian tradition. Mrs. Pearce conducts Eliza to "a spare bedroom" on "the third floor." Eliza had "expected to be taken down to the scullery," but she begins her transformation by a physical elevation that metaphorically parallels her expected rise in social stature. She is told "to make [herself] as clean as the room: then [she] wont be afraid of it"—a simile that counters the previous elevation metaphor with its continuation of the girl's dehumanization. Eliza associates cleanliness with death; however, the metaphoric, sexual sense of death remains perhaps subtextual:

> LIZA. You expect me to get into that and wet myself all over! Not me. I should catch my death. I knew a woman did it every Saturday night; and she died of it. . . . (*weeping*) . . . Its not natural: it would kill me. Ive never had a bath in my life.

Mrs. Pearce counters with inducements and slurs: "Well, dont you want to be clean and sweet and decent, like a lady? You know you cant be a nice girl inside if youre a dirty slut outside." The reasoning is the twisted logic of upper-class male seducers of lower-class women in eighteenth and nineteenth century romance: submit, succumb, and receive the outer embellishments of higher social status. The ambiguity of the term *slut,* which can mean either a physically dirty or morally questionable woman, stands out strongly; Eliza's claims of being a "good girl" are thrown into question by the alternative, sexual connotation of the label. This indeterminacy resonates with the link between physical cleanliness and sexual purity that is inverted by the scene's subtext into physical cleanliness and sexual defloration.

Despite Eliza's cries of protest, she is ordered to "take off all [her] clothes."

> Mrs. Pearce puts on a pair of white rubber sleeves . . . then takes a formidable looking long handled scrubbing brush and soaps it profusely with a ball of scented soap. Eliza comes back with nothing on but the bath gown . . . a piteous

spectacle of abject terror. . . . Deftly snatching the gown away and throwing Eliza down on her back . . . she sets to work with the scrubbing brush. Eliza's screams are heartrending.

The blatancy of these stage directions implies Shaw's cognizance of their implications. The phallic brush and cleansing ball are applied with the clinical coldness of the bath/laboratory's rubber gloves. That Eliza should be thrown on her back to be "cleaned," which in a bathtub would literally lead to drowning, cements the rape imagery, highlighting for the reader the symbolic interpretation over the literal. Using a female surrogate for the male rapist, Shaw again conceives of this lesbian encounter in a heterosexual context, in keeping with the late Victorian/Edwardian medical paradigm for a lesbian relation. But perhaps more important, he transfers the onus of sexual violence onto a woman, thereby safeguarding the gruff geniality of Higgins and ensuring his respectability at the same time that he fulfills the dark threat to Eliza that the play's opening dialogue foreshadows.

THE "RAPE" ON FILM

The film version, which facilitated the inclusion of this scene, graphically follows the outline of Shaw's directions, and creates a profoundly disturbing atmosphere on screen. At the start of the bath scene, Mrs. Pearce wraps herself in a sheet/apron (instead of the printed "sleeves") and promptly corners Eliza in the bathroom, trying to talk her into removing her clothes. She finally pushes Eliza out into the adjacent bedroom to change into a robe, leaving Mrs. Pearce alone. At this point, ominous music begins quietly, and almost like the witch whose broomstick has been alluded to earlier, she begins to mix bath salts in a tub that quickly foams with the appearance of a bubbling cauldron. Mrs. Pearce looks toward the bedroom door with a determined glint in her eye and picks up the scrubbing brush and soap. After another brief tangle getting Eliza to remove the robe—the camera having cut to Mrs. Pearce draping the bathroom mirror with a towel—Eliza is seen in the tub, screaming and struggling with Mrs. Pearce, who . . . has the other woman by the hair, grabbing hold of it to keep Eliza submerged in the bathwater. Interspersed with her genuinely "heartrending" screams, Eliza cries, "I've never done this kind of thing before, really I haven't. . . . No, Mrs. Pearce, no, don't . . . stop

it . . . this has never happened to me before . . . oh help, help
. . . I've never been . . . stop it . . . help." Amid her screams,
the camera cuts to a shot of Higgins and Pickering at the foot
of the stairs below. They are staring up at the sound of the
cries, and they exchange a bemused look. Higgins shrugs
and turns back into his study, while Pickering remains,
smirking. The camera cuts back to Eliza, still screaming,
eyes shut (to keep out soap), hand groping along the tile wall
of the tub. Her hand grasps hold of a handle, and suddenly
the shower head above explodes with a cascade of shooting
water. This ejaculatory conclusion to the scene clearly liter-
alizes the subtextually heterosexual paradigm controlling
the attack on Eliza.

Although the actors, screenwriters, and directors must be
credited for the overall production, Shaw's close involvement with the film implicates him in its creation and impact
as well. The thrust of this scene in particular is patently
clear; the "innocuous" bath barely masks the reality of female violation conveyed by the dialogue and action.

When Eliza reenters Higgins's study, Shaw provides a description for her as he would for a new, as yet unnamed character: "a dainty and exquisitely clean young Japanese lady in
a simple blue cotton kimono," and indeed she is unrecog-
nized by the other characters, with the exception of Mrs.
Pearce, who has conducted the transformation. Significantly,
Eliza cannot "see" herself in the mirror after the bath; she
cannot confront the new self that has been robbed of all ves-
tiges of her old identity, including a symbolic virginity.

When she finally comes into her own at the end of the
play, Higgins observes that she has "had a bit of [her] own
back," meaning a little revenge on him, but also suggesting
another interpretation. She has chosen to return to a life independent of Higgins and Pickering, thus reasserting some
of the original identity she had lost while at Wimpole Street.
She declines Higgins's offer to "adopt [her] as [his] daughter
and settle money on [her]," his attempt to formalize the
structure that has defined their relationship to date. Needless to say, his earlier suggestion that Mrs. Pearce adopt
Eliza has long been forgotten, and Eliza expresses no in-
debtedness to the housekeeper for any of her learning. Ultimately, Mrs. Pearce emerges as an alter image for Eliza:
what she might become were she to stay in Higgins's household, for the older woman has never been able to break free

of the hold Higgins has over her.

Eliza's announcement, "I'll marry Freddy, I will, as soon as I'm able to support him," seems a refreshingly feminist twist on the usual pattern of young female pupils' marrying men inferior in some way to their paternal teacher. But Shaw's "sequel" undermines this assertiveness, by showing Eliza's financial dependence on Pickering and emotional involvement with Higgins for years to come. Thus in the narrative resolving the conflicts of the play, Shaw reasserts literary control over the more balanced voices of the drama and removes the power Eliza seems to gain in her fight for independence. Eliza may not "like" her father-figures all that much, but Shaw makes it clear in his closing sentence that for her, they will always be "godlike."

CHAPTER 4

Reviews and Continuing Reception

An Early Review of *Pygmalion*

Desmond MacCarthy

According to Desmond MacCarthy, who wrote this review in 1914, *Pygmalion* is a clever, amusing, and exhilarating comedy that contains many serious themes. The central action of the play concerns the interaction between Higgins and his creation, Eliza. The vital act 4, in which Eliza becomes a lady and wants more out of life, is the most dramatic sequence in the play. Higgins is not merely a professor of linguistics: He represents all artists who devote their creative force to a work of art. Desmond MacCarthy (1877–1952) was an English critic and writer. A member of the famed Bloomsbury Group, which included such major authors as E.M. Forster and Virginia Woolf, MacCarthy served as the drama critic for the English paper the *New Statesman* from 1913 to 1944.

Pygmalion? It looked like a misnomer. The story of Mr. Shaw's play on the face of it was that of an artist who turns a live girl into a work of art, and then by a considerable effort of self-control refrains from falling in love with her! It is an exhilarating, amusing, and often a deep comedy, and it is admirably interpreted at His Majesty's. Like all good comedies, it is full of criticism of life; in this case criticism of social barriers and distinctions, of the disinterested yet ferocious egotism of artists, of genteel standards, of the disadvantages of respectability, of the contrast between man's sense of values and woman's, and of the complexity and misunderstanding which a difference of sex introduces into human relations, however passionately one of the two may resolve to sink the He and She. During the course of the story, light—and sometimes it is a penetrating ray indeed—is thrown into all these corners of life. I hardly know how to tackle a play which bristles with so many points, especially as I must confess that I am not certain I understood the play as a whole. Has it an idea or does it simply bristle? The merriment of intellectual antics is in it; the wit of penetration: 'the difference between a flower girl and a duchess is not how she behaves but how she is treated'—there is a good deal in that comment upon manners. Mr Doolittle (so admirably played by Mr [Edmund] Gurney) is Mr Shaw's most amusing achievement, in his Dickens [after English novelist Charles] vein of exaggeration. Doolittle . . . is the philosophy of 'the undeserving poor', incarnate and articulate. He does not exist; but he is sufficiently like a type to make one fancy Nature may have been aiming at him. All the minor characters are well drawn.

HENRY AND ELIZA

Henry Higgins is an extremely interesting study; Eliza is excellent, but she is interesting chiefly from her situation—a flower-girl who after six months' training at the hands of Higgins, the professor of phonetics, can be passed off in society as a lady. That, of course, is the story, the simple circumference of the play; but where does the centre of interest lie? In the relation between Pygmalion-Higgins and Eliza-Galatea? I thought so while I was in the theatre, and my feelings at the end of the play were in one sense highly flattering to the dramatist, to his power of entertaining and interesting, for when the curtain fell on the mutual explanations of this pair I was in a fever to see it rise on Acts VI and VII; I wanted to see those two living together; I wanted to get to the *point* which I conceived was still ahead. Afterwards I grasped what I now take to be the idea: there was point in the title *Pygmalion* after all; the statue did become alive; Acts II, III, and IV, during which Eliza was being moulded into a lady, were not the miracle, but merely the chipping of the statue itself from the rough block; but in Act V something happened, she had got a soul, and therefore the play was really over. I felt inclined, however, to credit myself with uncommon penetration when I discovered what had happened to Eliza in the fifth act. Perhaps when I read my fellow critics I shall discover that what I found with effort was quite obvious to them. In that case I retract in advance the criticism that Mr Shaw has huddled up his climax, and failed to arrange the perspective of the dialogue so that the mind is led easily up to the central point. Now the last act is, and is not, a love scene; Pygmalion-Higgins, like other Shavian heroes, is running away from passion, and Sir Herbert Tree acted admirably his nervousness, his dread of even touching Eliza lest the floods of irrational emotion should be released in himself. The experiment is over; it has been a triumph for his art as professor of phonetics; Eliza has passed through the stage of talking like a flower-girl with a mechanical meticulous pronunciation (Act III); she has become, both in the matter as well as the manner of her conversation, indistinguishable from a born lady; Higgins has won his wager. She has run away from him because she has found intolerable his tyranny and his disregard for her as a human being with feelings (Act IV). All along she has shown a spaniel-like docility and gratitude which he has never thought of recognising. He has fagged [British slang for "worked hard"] her about right and left; she has become useful, almost necessary to him in practical ways; but the more she tries to please and touch him the more harshly impersonal he becomes. But when she runs away he is frantic to get her back. The question is on what terms; he won't offer her anything more than he gave her before and does not understand at first that she only wants to be treated like a human being. Then she turns on him: threatens, to his dismay, to go off to his rival with all the secrets of his art; in short, shakes him off and stands on her own feet as an independent human being. The statue has become alive, during the six months' hard training she had acquired the outward signs of self-respect, but she never had the inward reality till this moment. Henceforward she is a person he can reckon upon, and his fear of her disappears. That I take it is the theme of the play.

HENRY AS ARTIST

Higgins is called a professor of phonetics, but he is really an artist—that is the interesting thing about him, and his character is a study of the creative temperament. We have met him before in an early novel by Mr Shaw; he is Mr Jack the composer in *Love Among the Artists*. The gesture with which Higgins flings money at Eliza in the first act after browbeating her, the chivalry and roughness of it, is a repetition of the scene at Paddington when Jack gives all the money he has in his pockets to Gwendolen to whom, by the bye, he also subsequently taught elocution, bullying her into perfection and bitterly disappointing and puzzling her by treating their relation, which had begun so romantically, as a sternly matter-of-fact impersonal one the moment she became his pupil. Jack thought only of the job in hand. If, on the one hand, he treated her as though she were a machine he had to get into order, on the other, when he had made her a fine actress he no more expected gratitude from her than he did from the paper on which he had written a sonata. Higgins behaves in the same way to Eliza. Like Jack he has a total disregard of people's feelings, he is outrageously inconsiderate, and yet he is most human. His impatience is the impatience of the artist who only asks Heaven for peace to devote himself to his work. Sir Herbert Tree's acting was delightful at all points where the comedy rests on the comedy of anyone so incapable of self-control as Higgins teaching deportment; he did not, I thought, bring out forcibly enough the violent sincerity of the character. The professor has that absolute self-dependence, that attractive combination of egotism and disinterestedness of artists with creative force in them.

THE DRAMA OF ACT IV

Act IV is the most dramatic of the five. The three of them have been out to a fashionable dinner; Eliza has been perfect. She is to all intents and purposes a *lady*. The two men begin talking, Eliza sits apart. They are triumphant and tired. What a grind it has been—oof! it's over *at last*, what a blessing, what a triumph! While they are talking like this in her presence, there she sits, stony, miserable, stunned (how good [the actress] Mrs Patrick Campbell was!); Higgins has not the smallest inkling of what all this drilling and training has cost Eliza herself, or how hard she has tried to learn. It has been hard enough work for him chipping the statue out of the block, but the marble itself has suffered more.

Pygmalion Has No Point

H.W. Massingham

Theater critic H.W. Massingham reviews a 1914 performance of *Pygmalion*, starring British actors Sir Herbert Beerbohm Tree as Henry Higgins and Mrs. Stella Patrick Campbell as Eliza. While enjoying the subject matter and interaction of the characters in the play, Massingham believes that Shaw misses the mark by letting the comedy dissolve into silliness, then become too stiff and serious. He also finds Higgins to be too cold a character, a "male brute" who uses Eliza and then discards her. Finally, Massingham complains that he does not understand the point of Shaw's play. If it is a piece of social criticism, its significance is lost on him. H.W. Massingham was editor of the English paper the *Nation*.

There must be something wrong about it, said Mr. Shaw in one of a rather scandalous series of interviews with himself which preceded the appearance of *Pygmalion*, or all the world would not be going to see it. Mr. Shaw was right. There *is* something wrong about *Pygmalion*. To begin with, it is not in the right place. His Majesty's Theatre is too big, and [the actor portraying Higgins] Sir Herbert Tree is too slow. Mr. Shaw's art deals in hard, brilliant surfaces and quick reactions. Above all, his mind is tangential, shooting at everything that flies. These qualities do not consort with Sir Herbert's deliberate manner and the broad imposing stage to which it is set. Mr. Shaw should be played quickly and lightly, not magnificently and grandiosely. But there is a fault in the piece as well as in its production. Let me try and show what it is.

Excerpted from H.W. Massingham, review of *Pygmalion* in *The Nation*, April 18, 1914.

THE PROBLEM WITH *PYGMALION*

Pygmalion was a royal artist (the breed, save for the Kaiser, is extinct) who fell in love with a statue of ivory that his hands had made. In pity of his case [Greek goddess] Aphrodite breathed life into the beautiful creature, and Pygmalion duly married it. The story, like all good stories, had a meaning. Its inventor was well aware of the fact that the artist is first and most in love with his art; and Mr. Shaw, being in the same line of business himself, is also familiar with it. He knows, too, that this art-passion is an exclusive and cruelly exacting attachment, which dehumanizes its victim, so much so that the Greeks figured [the pastoral god] Pan as 'half a beast,' and [British poet] Mrs. [Elizabeth] Browning, in a suggestive little poem, shows how the making of a poet usually involves the spoiling of a man. Not without a price does the reed which Pan hacks and trims for his piping become a divine instrument; its life with the other reeds has gone for ever.

This is what is the matter with Eliza Doolittle, of Covent Garden, who has fallen into the hands of Mr. Henry Higgins, Professor of Phonetics. Mr. Higgins's specialty has led him into the most daring experiment possible to a *virtuoso* of his type, the transformation of a Cockney flower-girl into a duchess. The feat was not quite so formidable as it looked, for Mr. Higgins's task was merely to transmute one kind of slang into another—the lisping, drawling sing-song of the slum into the equally flat dialect of the drawing-room. As for the girl herself, all that was necessary was to devitalize and disembody her—to turn something into nothing. These tasks Mr. Higgins duly accomplished. But he had forgotten one thing—that he was dealing with a human being, not with a cleverly constructed machine. So, when his flower-girl has passed the supreme tests of queening it at a dinner, a dance, and a garden-party, her awakening wrath, love, feeling, character, make him aware of the kind of metal which he has tried to fashion for his sport. Eliza Doolittle had passed her examination in fine-ladyship, but she has not ceased to be a woman. When she asks him for a share in life, and in his love and interest, for a future, an occupation, he would fling her back into the slums, or into the arms of the first husband that offers. He, Higgins, artificer in flesh and blood, has done with her. So the girl turns on her brutal trainer, and shows him the kind of man he is by way of inviting him to finish the job he began, and step out of his world of self-sufficing artistry to the common ways of mankind. This he half-consents to do, more, I am afraid, in the spirit of a blackmailed criminal than of a man of genius who has been caught out.

HIGGINS IS TOO COLD

Now, this is assuredly a good subject, well suited to Mr. Shaw's fashion of holding romance upside down, and giving Truth an air of cold repulsion. Indeed, Professor Higgins is a little like the self that Mr. Shaw likes to show to the world, much in the spirit of a shy man who hides his spirituality or his tenderness under a mask of coarseness or of gruff demeanor. What I complain of is that with his reserves and ironies, and by a certain caprice and waywardness of thought, Mr. Shaw has failed to show his audience precisely what he meant. His Professor Higgins is not merely a bully, a ramping, swearing boor; he is such a gross vivisector [experimenter on living creatures], that the finer conception of the artist . . . almost disappears. Perhaps this is what Mr. Shaw designed him to be. But this is surely a needless and painful defamation of the legend. The artist of the Greek fable is tenderly disguised as a lover; at his best, Pygmalion-Higgins is merely a diligent watcher of a test-tube. Is that a dramatic conception? It might have been; but it is not. Rather it points to the unguarded spot in Mr. Shaw's artistic armor. He observes too coldly; life's absurdity juts so sharply out from the mass as to obscure its beauty. He has hardly the patience even to chronicle affection; it is the clash of wits—the excitement of argument—that seems to interest him. . . . Conceiving *Pygmalion* in the proper spirit of serious comedy, he lets it slip into farce, stiffens it again with irony, and then jollies it up with a shower of verbal squibs and crackers. Thus, when Higgins and Eliza really come to business, it is to no fine issue. He becomes the average male brute, who has found a useful female drudge. She is well fitted to be his helpmate. But he wants no helpmate, only a slipper-warmer; he has his art. Or perhaps he does, in which case he is Higgins no longer. The audience must guess whether he loves her or she loves him, and what kind of blood flows in the veins of these queer, jangling creatures.

Equally wanting in firmness of conception and treatment is the minor key of Mr. Shaw's fancy. Eliza's father, Alfred

Doolittle, is almost a masterpiece, save that, like Galatea-Eliza, he talks rather than is. He, too, stands for an admirable idea—the rude anarchic living of the workman exchanged by a turn of fortune for 'middle-class morality,' ending up in a dolorous, long-deferred wedding at St. George's Anover Square. Here, again, Higgins has interfered in what was no business of his; he should have let this genial ruffian go his wicked ways. Is this what Eliza's transmogrification was meant to illustrate? Again, I failed to follow Mr. Shaw's line of thought, or to see it as dramatic development. Eliza was immensely amusing as she talked slum talk in primmest Lindley Murray, and answered Park Lane's courtesies with the terrible, if meaningless, adjective, bl——y. But she talks like a gramophone, not like a woman. 'What hast thou done with thy life?' asks the poet of himself. I ask Mr. Shaw what he has made of the soul of Eliza. For here was the grand opportunity of his drama—the coming to herself of this slip of the streets when she realizes the crime which a cold-blooded brute of a scientist had committed against her. Mr. Shaw may have meant to show that the rich can do nothing for the poor but leave them alone, and await the judgment of God on both. That would have been a powerful piece of criticism. Mr. Shaw hints but does not make it.

Pygmalion on Stage and Screen

Pat M. Carr

Early productions of *Pygmalion* were a smash hit as audiences delighted in the interplay between Henry Higgins and Eliza Doolittle. The element of love between the two protagonists was always present, contends Pat M. Carr, even though Shaw himself was not primarily interested in romance but rather in teaching lessons about society, linguistics, and, in particular, social class. Despite Shaw's insistence that Eliza would marry Freddy, Carr claims that various versions of the play suggest a romance between Eliza and Higgins. A 1970s production of the play in London asserted Eliza's independence more than previous versions, and it suggested that the final meeting of Eliza and Higgins was one of equals, not of a subservient girl crawling back to her domineering master. Pat M. Carr has taught at the University of Texas at El Paso.

Shaw wrote in the preface to the printed edition of the play:

> I wish to boast that *Pygmalion* has been an extremely successful play all over Europe and North America as well as at home. It is so intensely and deliberately didactic, and its subject is esteemed so dry, that I delight in throwing it at the heads of the wiseacres who repeat the parrot cry that art should never be didactic. It goes to prove my contention that art should never be anything else.

Shaw used as a model for Higgins, a contemporary philologist, Henry Sweet, one of the most irascible men Shaw knew, but critics are often fond of seeing Shaw himself as Higgins. For Higgins's values are indeed the values of the play, and the lessons Higgins teaches are those Shaw intended to teach with his own brand of didacticism. One of these is found in Higgins's first speech to the whining Eliza:

Excerpted from Pat M. Carr, *Bernard Shaw.* Copyright © 1976 by Frederick Ungar Publishing Co., Inc. Reprinted by permission of The Continuum International Publishing Group.

A woman who utters depressing and disgusting sounds has no right to be anywhere—no right to live. Remember that you are a human being with a soul and the divine gift of articulate speech: that your native language is the language of Shakespeare and Milton and The Bible: and dont sit there crooning like a bilious pigeon.

The inarticulate are always at a disadvantage, and Shaw dramatized the fact that those with illiterate speech patterns can never hope for any upward mobility. He was at the same time taking careful jabs at the upper classes who base all value judgments on speech and who type-cast a person by the language he speaks.

A Play About Growing Up

But, of course, the play is also concerned with that other Shavian favorite—Growing Up. Eliza is the pupil, Higgins, the mentor in the strictest sense. But while Higgins can teach Eliza what he knows about phonetics and speech, it is up to her to find alone her own "spark of divine fire" that Higgins, and Shaw, knew is the potential of everyone. She must find alone her own strength. And Eliza does. She does grow up to realize that she does not need Higgins. Higgins says, "No use slaving for me and then saying you want to be cared for: who cares for a slave?" Eliza becomes aware of the slave mentality of the female sex. She learns that demanding someone care for her merely because she cares for him is a commercial exchange. She learns that she is a human being with all the potential that implies. And, of course, Higgins then begins to admire her new strength and dignity.

A Problematical Love Story

In *Pygmalion*, Eliza has grown into a woman and thus the controversy of the ending comes into being. The stage version of the play ends with Higgins's complete assurance that Eliza will come back. In the printed text, however, Shaw added an epilogue of caution to those who would read his play as a boy-meets-girl comedy. He insisted that the growth itself was a happy ending and that the romance of the subtitle (he had called it "A Romance in Five Acts") came from the seemingly improbable transformation of Eliza:

> The rest of the story need not be shown in action, and indeed, would hardly need telling if our imaginations were not so enfeebled by their lazy dependence on the ready-mades and reach-me-downs of the ragshop in which Romance keeps its stock of "happy endings" to misfit all stories.

He then proceeded to tell the reader how Eliza marries Freddy, opens her flower shop with Freddy as an errand boy, and then fails at it because she has no business sense.

The theatergoers, of course, note the love story implicit in the title. They are not reading the epilogue but are blithely watching the expected ending of a comedy wherein order is restored. There is nothing more disorderly, in the cosmic sense, than a bachelor and a young woman who never get together. And Shaw could never sell the justness of his arrangement to his public.

Not that he tried all that hard.

When the critics and audiences raved about the wonderful tragedy [German playwright Bertolt] Brecht had wrought in *Mother Courage*—a play he had intended as a comedy— Brecht dashed home to rewrite the play. Not so Shaw. When the critics and the audiences happily received *Pygmalion* as a love story, he simply wrote a preface and added an epilogue, but didn't tamper with the play itself.

PYGMALION'S EARLY THEATRICAL HISTORY

Pygmalion was first presented in German at the Hofburg Theater, Vienna, on October 16, 1913, and then again at the Lessing Theater, Berlin, on November 1, 1913. By the time it got to London, Shaw could tell the press that it had already been a success in Berlin, Vienna, Stockholm, Prague, Warsaw, Budapest, and the German-speaking section of New York. Then he added: "There must be something radically wrong with it if it pleases everybody, but at the moment I cannot find what it is."

The first London production at His Majesty's Theater, on April 11, 1914, is perhaps still the most famous. It opened with Sir Herbert Beerbohn Tree as Higgins and Mrs. Patrick Campbell as Eliza and became Shaw's first fashionable theater run. The staging had realistic, cramped Victorian sets, and the costumes gave Mrs. Campbell ample chance to show her flair for style. Tree was one of the most famous English actor-managers, and Mrs. Campbell was the acknowledged English queen of melodrama. Both were a little too old and too heavy for the parts, and the *Daily Express* asked, "Where is youth these days?" and then answered:

> Far from being at the helm it is lucky to be allowed to scrub the decks. A new play is to be performed tonight at His Majesty's. The combined ages of its author, its leading lady

and its manager is 166. Sir Herbert is 60, Mr. Shaw is 57 and Mrs. Patrick Campbell, who plays a flower-girl of 18, is 49. The play was nonetheless a spectacular commercial success. The public still wanted to see two of England's great theatrical luminaries in the same play. The ending was, of course, interpreted romantically, and the audience was certain that the couple would get together. Tree, in fact, in the final scene, as Eliza went off to the wedding, took a bouquet from a table and tossed it with a kiss out the window to her. The *Illustrated London News* even congratulated Shaw on his unusual "happy ending." Shaw was appalled. When he confronted Tree with the alteration, Tree said, "My ending makes money; you ought to be grateful." Shaw snorted, "Your ending is damnable; you ought to be shot."

THE FILMS

Pygmalion was one of Shaw's most popular plays all over the world, but after the 1938 British film version, it was even more popular. This was the third filmed version of the play—there had been a German one in 1935, directed by Erich Engel, and a Dutch version in 1937, directed by Ludwig Berger. The English version was done by Gabriel Pascal, his first film of a Shaw play, and starred Leslie Howard as Higgins and Wendy Hiller as Eliza.

Shaw wrote the screenplay for the film, and added the scene of Eliza's triumph at the party in this version, the *scène à faire* being easier to accommodate in film than on stage. He said in an interview with the *Glasgow Evening Times* (February 7, 1939):

> As to *Pygmalion*, the scene in which Eliza makes her successful debut at the Ambassador's party was the root of the play at its inception. But when I got to work I left it to the imagination of the audience, as the theatre could not afford its expense and it made the play too long. Sir James Barrie [a long-time friend and neighbor of Shaw's] spotted this at once and remonstrated. So when the play was screened, I added the omitted scene, as the cinema can afford practically unlimited money, and the absense of intervals left plenty of time to spare.

Shaw had originally envisioned Charles Laughton in the role of Higgins and wrote a new ending especially for him. Of course, no Eliza could get romantically involved with the moon-faced, middle-aged Laughton, who had already established himself as the perfect Captain Bligh [in the film *Mutiny on the Bounty*]. Thus, this version, which was never filmed, shows Higgins on the street beside the cab in which Freddy has come to take Eliza to the wedding. He sees a flashback of Eliza in the mud the way he saw her first, then sees a flashforward of her in a flower shop with Freddy. Then the cab drives away, Higgins looks after it, and a policewoman asks, "Anything wrong, sir?" He says with crisp dignity as he walks off down the street: "No, nothing wrong. A happy ending. A happy ending. Good morning, madam."

But the handsome romantic lead, Leslie Howard, was given the part instead, and Pascal ended the film as Eliza comes back to the apartment and Higgins says, "Eliza, where are my slippers?" Pascal knew how Shaw felt about romantic interpretations of his play, and he waited with great trepidation as the film ended. Shaw said nothing, but as the lights came on, a faint smile appeared on his face. He let Pascal's ending stand without reproach almost as if he, too, subconsciously wanted romance as much as his public.

THE MUSICAL

In 1956 came the musical version, *My Fair Lady*. Shaw had been adamant during his lifetime about not allowing his plays to be adapted as musicals after he saw the debacle of *The Chocolate Soldier*, which was made in 1909 from *Arms and the Man*. After Shaw's death, however, Pascal had approached all the big names in musical comedy from Cole Porter to Noel Coward and the Richard Rodgers–Oscar Hammerstein team to see if *Pygmalion* could be adapted for the musical stage. All refused. The play was not really a love story, and everyone knew the original play could not be tampered with too much. Then Alan Lerner and Frederick Loewe agreed to the adaptation. They added and enlarged the climactic ball scene and changed the afternoon tea (Act III) at Mrs. Higgins's to a box at the Ascot races. In this scene, aware that the American audience might not fully appreciate the impact of [the vulgar English word] "bloody," they altered Eliza's faux pas of "Not bloody likely" to her shout at the horse, "Move your bloomin' arse."

Moss Hart directed the play and achieved an old-fashioned elegance combined with 1920's extravagant glitter. Many of Shaw's words were incorporated into the songs, and Doolittle's two production numbers, "With a Little Bit of Luck" and

"Get Me to the Church on Time," utilized the music-hall quality Shaw saw in the original character of Doolittle and effectively summarized in music his Shavian philosophy. The ending of the musical was that of the 1938 film.

The musical became internationally popular, and four years after it opened on Broadway, it was playing simultaneously in London, Oslo, Stockholm, Melbourne, Copenhagen, and Helsinki.

A MORE BALANCED *PYGMALION*

[A more] recent production of the original *Pygmalion*, without the song and dance, was that at the Albery Theater, London, which opened May 16, 1974, with Diana Rigg and Alex McGowen. As Irving Wardle commented in the *London Times* (May 17, 1974): "Great musical though it was, *My Fair Lady* has much to answer for in keeping this masterpiece off the stage for so long. And among the pleasures of John Dexter's magnificent revival (the first in the West End since 1953) is that of rediscovering how musical Shaw's own work is without any outside assistance."

Wardle liked especially the production's development of Eliza into a strong match for Higgins: ". . . at the end they are two of a kind, such perfectly matched partners that it hardly matters whether they share a house or not." He saw that a pair of actors had worked out the balanced male-female roles that Shaw intended.

Jeremy Kingston of *Punch* (May 29, 1974) added:

> Unlike the Greek legendary original it is the statue that falls in love with Pygmalion. Dexter minimizes the romantic content of this love and adds to Shaw's original unsentimental ending a firmly slammed door for Eliza to emphasize her independence. Versions in which she creeps back to Higgins's flapping slippers achieve this fatuous happy ending only by turning the characters into barley sugar. Independence is the theme.

Perhaps for the first time, we have an audience ready for independent males and females and for the balanced male-female relationship Shaw intended when he first wrote the play.

Pygmalion: From Play to Motion Picture

Donald P. Costello

In this selection, Donald P. Costello explains how two unsuccessful motion pictures had been made from Shaw plays before producer Gabriel Pascal succeeded where others had failed. By gaining major concessions from the playwright, his 1938 film, *Pygmalion*, had numerous new and altered scenes amounting to 37 percent of the film's playing time. According to Costello, Pascal's adaptation of Shaw's play allowed for full use of emerging cinematic techniques that enhanced the production. The motion picture was a rousing success, celebrated by moviegoers and critics alike on both sides of the Atlantic. Donald P. Costello has taught at the University of Notre Dame. He has authored books on George Bernard Shaw's movies and on film director Federico Fellini.

In 1937 a statement signed by Bernard Shaw appeared in a motion-picture trade journal: "We are to have a British *Pygmalion* film presently. Pascal Films have announced it. Wait and see. At all events, this time it will be an authentic Shaw screen version." Behind that "authentic Shaw screen version" lies a tale, a tale of a three-year tug of war between two mighty wills and two mighty egos. Shaw and Pascal worked with one another and against one another, but they were united in purpose in one mighty crusade: to bring Shaw to the cinema.

THE HUNT FOR MONEY

After that "auspicious day" when Gabriel Pascal received from Bernard Shaw the cinema rights to *Pygmalion*, the penniless Hungarian all but moved heaven and earth to get the work of the Master on the screen. His first problem was a financial one. The money did not begin pouring in the moment Shaw signed the contract. Pascal had the job of getting money from financiers who remembered only too well the financial disasters which had struck the backers of Shaw's two previous filmed plays. No one, of course, had confidence that Pascal would be able to squeeze, charm, and pressure enough changes out of Shaw to make *Pygmalion* an acceptable film. Columbia Pictures wrote Pascal that they could enter into contract only if they could "have the right to make changes in the scenario and to omit portions thereof and make alterations therein, to transpose parts of the same and interpolate therein parts of other works; And that we shall have the right to recut, re-edit and reassemble and reconstruct said photoplay in such manner as we in our sole discretion shall deem advisable." Shaw, it need hardly be mentioned, said "No."

Eventually, others joined Pascal in the hunt for money. They heard objections that nobody was interested in the classics, that Pascal was too inexperienced, that Shaw would never cooperate in the necessary adaptations, that *Pygmalion* didn't have enough sex to become a successful film. But a financier named Nicholas Davenport formed a syndicate among friends of his in London and managed, in spite of the objections, to get together 10,000 pounds. Richard Norton, the head of Pinewood Studios, used his vast influence to round up backers. A successful flour miller named J. Arthur Rank was just getting interested in films and decided to add his support. Finally, production was arranged at Pinewood Studios in England, with Gabriel Pascal as producer, and with a young director named Anthony Asquith, who had not yet made his mark on the cinematic world, sharing the direction of the film with actor Leslie Howard. Loews was signed to become the American distributor. But financial matters never were serene. Throughout production, *Pygmalion* clung tenuously to life, threatened every day with financial collapse.

THE ACTORS

Casting was not nearly so big a problem as money. Shaw at first told Pascal that he should pay a visit to Covent Garden and pick, for Eliza, the first flower girl he came across. But, in a more serious mood, Shaw had seen a new young actress named Wendy Hiller in a play called *Love on the Dole;* he saw her as the perfect Eliza. "This is your fate," Pascal later told her. "I will make you famous." Pascal was determined to have Leslie Howard as Henry Higgins, but Shaw was suspicious of Howard's screen image as a romantic idol. "The public will like him and probably want him to marry Eliza," said Shaw, "which is just what *I* don't want." Shaw wanted, instead, a determined antiromantic in the role, and even suggested that Leslie Howard, who was "hopelessly wrong," should change roles with Cecil Trouncer, a villain-type stage actor who was cast for the small new role of a constable. But Pascal, in the first of his many victories over Shaw, signed Leslie Howard both to play Professor Higgins and to co-direct the film. Romance had won its first round. Bit parts were all filled by Pascal with unusual care and extravagance. A first glimmering of that unconcern for money which was eventually to get Pascal into much trouble now shone through: "I hired the very best actors in London," boasted Pascal, "even for extra roles. Instead of two pounds a day I paid them fifteen. And I told them, 'All right, it is an honor for you to be an extra in a Shaw picture.'"

SHAW'S BIGGEST CONCESSION

But both money and personnel were, after all, only preliminaries. The central problem was the one that persisted throughout all of Shaw's connections with the cinema: How much would the movie depart from the play? Who would win the battle, Shaw or the film makers? "Our understanding," wrote Pascal, "was that I should put his plays on the screen as they were." Shaw wrote confidently: "Mr. Gabriel Pascal will produce the author's scenario." Shaw insisted, of course, that no additions or omissions be made in that scenario without his express permission. But the difference between *Pygmalion* and the previous Shaw films was precisely that—permission *was* given. A neighbor of Shaw's, who had many conversations with him about the making of the film, exclaimed in surprise: "He agreed to almost all of Pascal's suggestions!" "What Gabby did," Blanche Patch [Shaw's secretary] has written, "was to persuade Shaw to make the play presentable in the new medium. It was the biggest concession Shaw ever made to anyone."

The assembled hordes collected by Gabriel Pascal descended upon Shaw, pressuring him constantly for changes and adaptations. He complained that Pascal's studio was "immediately infested with script writers" and with "about twenty directors who spent their time trying to sidetrack me and Mr. Gabriel Pascal." This attempt to get changes out of Shaw was ticklish business, not for the faint of heart. Leslie Howard's daughter recalls that "the script writers walked on eggs when trying to cut or change any part of the dialogue." Anthony Asquith was awarded the first major encounter: he had the job of convincing Shaw to write a ballroom scene showing Eliza's triumph, a climax which never actually appeared on the stage. Asquith succeeded. But, predictably, the most effective concession-getter was Pascal himself. "I went to' GBS [George Bernard Shaw]," Pascal said, "and told him I needed several changes. He smiled and started his Irish fight; and I started my Hungarian fight; and I think the Hungarian is more effective than the Irish because I won."

Although Shaw wrote, under pressure, much of the additional material for the film version of *Pygmalion*, the script of the film was certainly not totally his work. The first script was, in fact, not actually written by Shaw but by his former director, Cecil Lewis. Mr. Lewis . . . wrote to me: "I wrote the original script of *Pygmalion* in Hollywood. It was later rewritten by W.P. Lipscomb and others." "There has been more tinkering with *Pygmalion*," wrote Blanche Patch, "than with any other work of his." The final script did, however, have the approval of Shaw, and he even appeared on the screen in a spoken preview introducing the finished film to the audiences of the movie theatres.

As Shaw did not so completely control the script of *Pygmalion* as he did with both his previous and subsequent films, so he did not so completely control the production. But, being Shaw, he did insist on a strong advisory capacity. Pascal and I, he said, "are in business together. He doesn't move a step without my advice." Still photos of the production were sent to Shaw throughout the filming, and he managed to assert considerable influence over even minute details through his comments. "I showed him the still photos weekly," Pascal wrote, "and he immediately recognized with his critical eye the development of the characters by the players. He saw the slightest faults in their make-up or in their portrayal, or the slightest error in sets and decor, and he became my second artistic conscience." But Shaw was a far-away conscience to Pascal, and thus not a very troublesome one. Shaw visited the studio only to see the opening shots. "I don't propose to interfere in the direction of the picture," Shaw wrote to Pascal, "since I cannot, at my age, undertake it myself." Pascal, Asquith, and Howard were thus relatively free to be film makers.

Only an examination of the changes which *Pygmalion* underwent in its journey from stage to screen will show just how startling were the concessions that Pascal was able to wring from Shaw. . . . Pascal knew that if the motion picture *could* depart from the restrictions of the stage, the audience would demand that it do so. A work of art is expected to move about freely within its own limitations, not to assume the limitations of another medium. Pascal was out to adapt *Pygmalion* to the motion picture medium, not to repeat the filmed-play disasters of [Shaw's plays] *How He Lied to Her Husband* and *Arms and the Man.* The medium of the motion picture itself controlled the demands which Pascal, Anthony Asquith, and Leslie Howard made upon Shaw.

NEW MATERIAL

The most obvious difference between the screen version and the play version of *Pygmalion* is the large amount of new material written especially for the screen. Shaw himself admitted that Pascal talked him into writing "all the new scenes that the screen makes possible and that are impossible in the theatre." These new scenes numbered fourteen, plus a written prologue. . . .

These fourteen new scenes represent a considerable total quantity of new material. Shaw's insistence that a movie could simply reproduce a play as it had appeared on the stage had been modified by his later admission that events which for practical reasons had to take place offstage could effectively be represented on the screen. Indeed, this admission brought into the film of *Pygmalion* new visual scenes which occupied thirty-one and a half minutes, out of a total playing time of eighty-five minutes. These new visualizations in the screen version of *Pygmalion* thus account for 37 per cent of the film's entire playing time.

The professional film makers who created the actual film of *Pygmalion* from a script which Shaw worked on and approved saw to it that this was not a mere recorded play. . . . In addition to the fact that over one third of the film consisted of new material, many other changes prove the fact that this *Pygmalion* exploited many filmic possibilities which the stage, of course, could not offer.

CINEMATIC TECHNIQUES

The film contains a good deal of visual material accompanying the dialogue, the filmic counterpart to "stage business." The film exploits the visual possibilities of this "stage business," however, for many effects which the stage, far-away, at a constant distance, without visual dynamism, could never duplicate. The film combines elements of spectacle and movement, speed and surprise, and musical and lighting virtuosity to create a visual excitement which parallels the emotional and intellectual excitement at such climactic scenes as Eliza's lessons and Eliza's triumph at the Ball; but the film also creates a visual excitement throughout, at less climactic moments, as the camera races about, often blurring in its speed, as it tries to keep up with a restless Higgins who is often chasing after a fearful Eliza, a restless Higgins who is always pacing, always playing with objects in his hands, paper-weights, apples, vases. This motion is compounded over stage motion, for when Higgins moves, the camera moves to keep up with him, and the observer has the illusion that he himself is moving. Motion is even more dramatically felt through the technique of cutting, as the observer constantly changes the distance and angle of his vantage point.

The cinema's increased powers of visualization accompanying the dialogue are used in *Pygmalion* for increased humor as well as for increased dynamism. This use of visual humor is shown most obviously in the famous tea-party scene at the home of Mrs. Higgins, the scene which provides Eliza with her first test. The wonderfully prim artificiality of the situation is established at the very beginning, with a lingering close-up of Clara Eynsford Hill and Eliza shaking hands by daintily rubbing two of their fingers together. Throughout the scene, all of Eliza's remarks are greeted with close-shots of varying facial reactions to her shocking sentences, subtle reactions which the stage could not force us to see. The scene is filled with long silent pauses while everyone frantically stirs his tea and we watch their faces. Thus, when the subject of weather comes up and Eliza adds two *new* lines—"The rain in Spain, they say, stays mainly in the plain," and "In Hampshire, Hereford, and Hartford, hurricanes hardly ever happen"—the camera slowly pans from face to bewildered face during an excruciatingly long pause, longer certainly than could have been maintained with interest on the stage. Similarly, when Eliza says, ". . . but my father he kept ladling gin down her throat till she came to so sudden that she bit the bowl off the spoon" we are treated to close-shots of both the exasperated Pickering and the shocked Vicar. Eliza's own later discomfiture is communicated by the close-shot of her puzzled face as she finds herself crippled with a cup in one hand and a plate in the other. After she finally gets rid of her plate, her frantic effort to succeed is shown by her imitating the whirlwind tea-stirring of the other guests, and by her holding out *all* her fingers, instead of just the little one, as she tries to drink. Finally, when Higgins signals Eliza that it is time to leave, she coolly replaces on the serving tray her half-eaten sandwich, as the camera catches the bulging eyes of Mrs. Eynsford Hill.

Much of the close-up visual humor is more fleeting than in the tea-party scene. Throughout the scene of Doolittle's first appearance, for example, he continually wheezes, as the others back away reeling from the smell, with expressions of utter asphyxiation on their faces. Mrs. Pearce at one time snatches a box of chocolates away from Higgins with the disapproving look of a den mother.

CAMERA ANGLES

A third function is served by visual additions acting as an accompaniment to the dialogue: subtle editorial comments can be made by the position of the camera. It is an old cinematic trick to shoot a character from a high angle when he is dominated, to shoot him from a low angle when he is dominating. Thus, a very low camera and some dark shadows—a good exploitation of creative lighting as well as creative camera angle—make Doolittle very imposing, even frightening, when he says at his first appearance, "I come about a very serious matter, Governor." The most interesting camera-angle editorial comments are those which silently comment on the changing Higgins-Eliza relationship. When Higgins decides, "I shall make a duchess of this draggle-tailed guttersnipe," he stands over Eliza, as the camera shoots him from her angle, Higgins towering majestically high. When he tells her the conditions of her stay, "If you're naughty and idle you will sleep in the back kitchen among the black beetles. . . ," he not only is shot from a low angle, but he even walks partway up the stairs so as to get still higher. And the ultimate step in camera angle as editorial commentator comes when Higgins says to Eliza, "If you refuse this offer you will be a most ungrateful and wicked girl," and he walks in front of her, blotting her completely out of view. The worm turns when finally, toward the end of the movie, Eliza asserts her newly found independence from Higgins. Then *she* is shot from a low angle, and she becomes the towering figure. . . .

NECESSARY CHANGES

Many of the minor omissions and replacements in the screen version of *Pygmalion* were due not to the intrinsic nature of the film medium but were due to external circumstances of the cinema industry. Lines and situations were changed because somewhere on the globe someone might have been offended: the film, as Shaw had pointed out, had to, for profit reasons, "go around the world unchallenged." Thus, for example, the language of *Pygmalion* on the screen is less explosive than the language of *Pygmalion* on the stage. All of Higgins's frequent damnings are deleted, and Freddy's "Damnation!" is changed to "O blast!" Mrs. Pearce's comment about Eliza not wanting to be a "dirty slut" is changed to "dirty girl," and Higgins does not call Eliza a "damned impudent little slut." Eliza does still use her "scarlet expletive," which had caused a major scandal when the play was first produced in London in 1914. But by 1938 the impact of "Not bloody likely" had so weakened that it no longer created a sensation, not even in the sensitive movies. *My Fair Lady,* incidentally, to get the desired impact from Eliza's social gaucherie found it necessary to substitute Eliza's "move your bloomin' arse," spoken at the Ascot races. The sexually scandalous, too, was deleted from the film: Doolittle never mentions that he isn't married, and so Eliza does not tell Mrs. Pearce, as she did in the play, "Her that turned me out was my sixth step-mother"; and so, also, . . . all the lines referring to Doolittle's coming marriage are deleted from the final scenes. . . .

Some of the most significant differences between the play and the film are caused by this cinematic tendency toward simplification. Several hundred lines of dialogue are cut, whole pages are lost, in an effort to narrow the story, to concentrate on the Eliza-Higgins relationship. Just as the additions tended to emphasize the Eliza-Higgins theme, so do the omissions. Doolittle's lines are the ones which are most severely cut, . . . Not only details about Doolittle's background are lost, but also much of his Shavian philosophy about middle-class morality. As Doolittle's class consciousness is weakened, so is Higgins's. He does not say, for example, "Don't you know that a woman of that class looks a worn out drudge of fifty a year after she's married?" nor does he tell Eliza that as a common girl she has no possible future.

Light chatter that is nonessential to the basic Eliza-Higgins relationship, no matter how filled this dialogue is with Shavian paradox, is eliminated from the severely cut tea-party scene. And the subtleties of the Eliza-Higgins debate in the last act, again filled with Shavian paradox, are freely cut. . . .

As the social dimension of *Pygmalion* is weakened, the romantic Cinderella-like story is correspondingly strengthened. Even certain characteristics of both Higgins and Eliza are altered so as to make them more immediately attractive, more fitting as a romantic pair. Higgins is made less violent and harsh than he was in the play. He simply says to Eliza, "A woman who utters such depressing and disgusting sounds has no right to be anywhere"; he does not add, as he did in the play, "no right to live." He does not shout, "Give her orders: that's enough for her." His antiwoman and antimarriage speeches are omitted, and so is his devotion to his mother. Eliza, as a flower girl, is not quite so crude as in the play. The lines about her not knowing what to do with her handkerchief are cut, and so are those in which Mrs. Pearce makes clear the necessity of burning Eliza's hat. And Eliza, as a lady, is made even more attractive in the film because we have *seen* Freddy's devotion to her and, most significantly, her great triumph at the Ball. Later, Eliza's snobbery about attending her father's wedding is conveniently eliminated, as all references to Doolittle's nonmarried state are cut. What remains, after a great deal of omission, is the clear and simple situation of a Galatea finally being fully created by her Pygmalion, finally asserting her own individual soul, and, becoming independent, being free to choose. She chooses Higgins.

In transferring *Pygmalion* to the screen, then, Shaw allowed, as he had earlier forbidden, "transpositions, interpolations, omissions, and alterations." The finished film, with much added and much left out and much changed from the play, opened at the Leicester Square Theatre in London on October 6, 1938. Ignoring the changes, Shaw wrote to Pascal: "You have had a tremendous triumph, on which I congratulate you and myself." Shaw was as happy with his new Eliza as he was with the triumphant new film. He told Wendy Hiller: "You've nearly wiped my old play off the map." The triumph soon spread from London to the rest of England. Mrs. Patrick Campbell [the stage actress who first played Eliza] wrote to Shaw:

> From a friend I heard of the huge success of *Pygmalion* at the Odeon Theatre, Chesterfield, with a population of twenty-three thousand, and there were twenty-one thousand seats sold in the week. And I hear that the miners came in their rough clothes straight from the mine and enjoyed every word of your wit. And you on a percentage! You must be making more money than you know what to do with.

After working out some details with Loews, Inc., for the American distribution of *Pygmalion*, Pascal travelled to New York to witness a similar American triumph. "*Pygmalion* was a revolution from the first day in New York, understand me?" Pascal reported. "On the first day on Broadway it was two blocks the queue." In city after city, *Pygmalion* broke American box-office records. An astonished *Variety* piled up the adjectives—"big," "surprise," "strong," "hot," "smash"— as the film moved across America. *Variety* finally called *Pygmalion* "one of the wonders of post-depression Broadway" and "the Gibraltar of pictures." Pascal concluded:

> America does not want little monkey stories, because they have plenty little monkeys there themselves. Everyone there is crazy for Bernard Shaw. His are not little monkey stories, you see? Understand me?

From Hollywood, Pascal wrote to Shaw: "You are a greater boxoffice star here than their Greta Garbo."

Pygmalion's success soon grew to international proportions, as it filled theatres in Canada, South Africa, Australia, and, finally, Continental Europe.

Although financial figures are a well-guarded motion picture industry secret, there is no doubt that *Pygmalion*, which at a modest $675,000 managed to keep within its preproduction budget, was a tremendous box-office success. (The film even repeated its financial triumph when it was rereleased in 1944, and again in 1949.) Pascal and Shaw did, indeed, reap a rich harvest on *Pygmalion*, but Shaw contended that the film's financial success backfired:

Suppose you have a film success and receive £20,000 for the first time in your life! That is what happens at best. Immediately you are taxed 19s 6d [19 shillings and 6 pence] in the pound not only on the £20,000 but on your ordinary earnings as well. That is, you collect money for the war and get a commission of sixpence in the pound, which does not pay for the overhead. In short, you are a ruined man, as I am at this moment, thanks to the colossal success of *Pygmalion.*

The box-office success of *Pygmalion* was aided by the critics, who, as a full-page advertisement in *Variety* put it, "fan the blaze with plaudits everywhere." *The Motion Picture Review Digest* counted 112 reviews—111 favorable, and one mixed. Out of nine New York newspapers, eight critics placed *Pygmalion* on their lists of "The Year's Ten Best." Shaw won the Academy Award for the "best screen play of the year." (He later commented about the Oscar: "It's not *real* gold; it's just a sham.") W.P. Lipscomb, Cecil Lewis, and Ian Dalrymple won the Academy Award for the best "adaptation." The National Board of Review gave a special commendation to the performance of Wendy Hiller as Eliza.

What had the phenomenal critical and financial success of the film version of *Pygmalion* proved? What had been proved about Shaw's theory of the cinema? The play had been extensively adapted, both in accord with some important intrinsic demands of the medium and with the external circumstances of movie profit, when in this pull and tug between Shaw and Pascal it was moved from stage to screen. Shaw had certainly been proved wrong in his contention that a play could without adaptation be successfully moved to the cinema: a comparison between the play and the actual film proves that this successful Shaw-Pascal *Pygmalion* was certainly not merely a filmed play, as the disastrous *How He Lied to Her Husband* and *Arms and the Man* had been.

A Successful Adaptation

But was the *Pygmalion* film a distinctive art, a true motion picture? The answer is that the Shaw-Pascal film was neither a pure play nor a pure film; it was something in between. It was not a pure play—no successful film could ever be. It was not a pure film, for it was not, as cinema aestheticians demand, originally conceived and worked out in visual terms. It was neither pure play nor pure film; it was, instead, all that it hoped to be: a successfully adapted motion picture version of a Shaw play.

Pygmalion Becomes *My Fair Lady*

Hollis Alpert

According to Hollis Alpert, with a push from Gabriel Pascal, who had brought *Pygmalion* to film, the writing team of Alan Jay Lerner and Frederick "Fritz" Loewe constructed a musical that preserved much of George Bernard Shaw's original intent while still adapting the play to a new genre. With its lively songs and impressive cast, the musical version of *Pygmalion*, called *My Fair Lady*, was an instant Broadway smash and has been called by one critic "the greatest musical of the twentieth century." Hollis Alpert has served as film critic and senior editor at the *Saturday Review*. He has written more than a dozen works of fiction and nonfiction, including biographies of film celebrities such as Federico Fellini, Richard Burton, and the Barrymores.

Gabriel Pascal, a film producer, who was once described as "a swarthy adventurer from Transylvania," had a dream of making a musical from George Bernard Shaw's *Pygmalion*. When he approached Alan Jay Lerner and Frederick Loewe in 1952 to do the conversion, he told them they were the only people who could possibly realize his dream. This, Lerner and Loewe knew, was a Transylvanian exaggeration. Word was about that he had told much the same thing to [songwriters] Noël Coward, Cole Porter, E.Y. Harburg, and Rodgers and Hammerstein, all of whom turned down the "unique" opportunity.

INITIAL DIFFICULTIES

Lerner and Loewe were interested enough to work on an adaptation for three months before giving up, because, they realized, the play was basically drawing-room comedy, and turning it to musical form would entail doing violence to Shaw's structure. Two years later they tried again, but Pascal died, creating a confused legal situation. Lerner and Loewe went on working, hoping the rights' difficulties would be clarified. By then they had decided it would do no great harm to Bernard Shaw (also gone from this earth) if the audience was told what happened between the scenes of the play's five acts. In this way, characters only mentioned in the play could be brought to life and the show could become more populous. Eliza Doolittle, the cockney flower-seller whose accent and language so bothered Professor Higgins, would go home and see her dustman father, Doolittle, before appearing at Higgins's house the next day for her speech improvement. In the play the audience never saw the pronunciation lessons; Lerner and Loewe decided to use them. The tryout of Eliza's newly acquired cultural wings would not occur at a tea party, but would afford more dramatic possibilities at fashionable Ascot [a horse-racing track].

CASTING THE PLAY

With Pascal gone, a producer was found in Herman Levin, who had shepherded *Call Me Mister* and *Gentlemen Prefer Blondes* to successful runs. Almost from the moment they began working, Lerner and Loewe had made the decision that they wanted Rex Harrison for the querulous Professor Higgins, in spite of his lack of a traditional singing voice. As Lerner related about the musical's development stage, "It would strain the credulity of the audience if Professor Higgins suddenly opened his mouth and poured forth a rich baritone."

In February 1955, by which time Lerner and Loewe had written seven songs for what they were then calling "My Lady Liza," they flew to London to convince Harrison he was the ideal Henry Higgins. It wasn't easy. It was "hard for Rex to reach a decision," Lerner said of him. "He studied a menu for twenty minutes before ordering his soup." But Rex finally capitulated, after being told songs would be written for him to sing in a nonsinging way.

Harrison, without a powerful voice, represented a new concept of a leading man in a musical play. "The trick was," Lerner related, "to write the lines for music exactly the way a nonsinging person says them. Once we'd done that, Rex could either say them or sing them, and all would be well." In the case of the Higgins song "I've Grown Accustomed to

Her Face," Loewe wrote it the way a normal person would say the lines instead of singing them, with no drawn-out notes for any of the words.

At forty-one, Mary Martin was old for the role of Eliza, but nonetheless indicated her interest in playing it. Lerner and Loewe met with her and her husband and played five of the songs they had written, among them the "Ascot Gavotte," and

---

ELIZA BECOMES A CENTRAL FOCUS THROUGH SONG

Lerner and Loewe characterize Eliza Doolittle using simple lyrics in two songs from My Fair Lady.

Lerner and Loewe were sitting around talking about the song they'd need for Eliza's elocution lesson. Alan Jay Lerner suggested they use one of the exercises she'd been learning—'In Hartford, Hereford, and Hampshire, hurricanes hardly happen' or perhaps 'The rain in Spain stays mainly on the plain.' Fritz Loewe liked the latter: 'Good, I'll write a tango,' he said, and completed the tune within ten minutes The combination of the words and music—humdrum repeat-after-me phrases set to exotic Spanish rhythms—makes it a novel and theatrical button for the scene.

Later in *My Fair Lady,* when Eliza has been successfully passed off as a duchess at the Embassy ball, she and Higgins and Colonel Pickering return home in joyous mood. Pickering offers congratulations:

Tonight, old man, you did it!

You did it! You did it!

You said that you would do it

And indeed you did!

The scene has the same zest and glee and infectiousness as 'The Rain in Spain'. Pickering and Higgins have triumphed—and the notey, jittery tune and monosyllables emphasize their excitement. And then we notice that the one person who isn't singing is Eliza: the one who *really* did it. The song continues, but, instead of seeming celebratory, it now underlines their selfishness and insensitivity. We realize Eliza isn't a lump of clay—a chaps' wager. This is the moment in the drama when Lerner and Loewe shift the play's point of view, and our sympathies, from Higgins to Eliza.

And it all takes place during the song.

Mark Steyn, *Broadway Babies Say Goodnight.* New York: Routledge, 1999.

"Just You Wait" (Henry Higgins), none of which she liked.

The next choice was Julie Andrews, a charming nineteen-year-old who had appeared in *The Boy Friend*, an imported British pastiche about the twenties. She was close to Eliza in age, and had a lovely soprano voice, but she was kept waiting until no other important star possibility turned up. Meanwhile, Stanley Holloway, of English music-hall and musical-comedy fame, was tapped for Doolittle.

Moss Hart agreed to become the director as soon as he heard [the song] "Why Can't the English?" Cecil Beaton designed elegant Edwardian costumes; Oliver Smith created the sets, one of them a stunning Ascot enclosure in black, gray, and white; and Hanya Holm signed on as choreographer. William Paley, the head of CBS, through Goddard Lieberson, of the same company's record division, became interested enough to propose backing the entire show, a quid pro quo being that Columbia Records would have the rights to the original cast album.

In spite of the tinkering done to the text by Lerner, the musical, now named *My Fair Lady*, stayed remarkably close to the play, even to much of its dialogue. Nary a kiss was exchanged, as in Shaw's version, and the only slight deviation was in the ending, similar to that of the 1938 movie, which Shaw had allowed. The audience could feel that, if nothing else, the relationship between Higgins and Eliza would continue.

THE GREATEST MUSICAL OF THE TWENTIETH CENTURY

During the tryout, word spread that a magical new hit was working its way toward Broadway. By its mid-March 1956 opening, long lines had been forming at the Mark Hellinger Theatre for three weeks. Mail orders for tickets flowed in so heavily that Lerner, Loewe, and everyone else concerned worried that too much was expected. There was no cause for worry. Walter Kerr called the show "miraculous," and Brooks Atkinson decided he had seen "the greatest musical of the Twentieth Century."

My Fair Lady continues to stand as a truly landmark musical, rightfully showered with awards. It established a new record by staying on Broadway for six and a half years. There was hardly a country in the world where the show did not play, and recordings of the show were made in the language of every country in which it was performed. For its

$400,000 investment, CBS made in the neighborhood of fifty million dollars.

The question has been asked often: Why the remarkable, long-lasting appeal of *My Fair Lady*? There are the songs, of course, graceful, witty, appropriate—"I Could Have Danced All Night," "On the Street Where You Live," and the riotous "The Rain in Spain"—which lingered on the charts for years. Qualities of effervescent wit, of style, and of taste were not necessarily guarantees of long-lasting popularity, nor was a literate story, or an intelligent, sense-making plot. All of these the show had in enough abundance to make it a succès d'estime [a success of esteem]. But the show's astounding success had to derive from a rare combination of the right talents coming together at the right time.

CHRONOLOGY

1852

George Carr Shaw and Lucinda Elizabeth Gurley marry.

1856

George Bernard Shaw is born on July 26.

1866

George Vandeleur Lee, Lucinda Shaw's music teacher, moves in with the Shaws.

1871

Shaw leaves school to become a clerk.

1873

Lucinda Shaw moves to London.

1876

Shaw moves to London.

1879

Shaw finishes his first novel, *Immaturity*.

1881

Shaw becomes a vegetarian.

1884

Shaw joins the Fabian Society.

1885

Shaw's father, George Carr Shaw, dies.

1886

George Vandeleur Lee dies.

1888

Shaw becomes the music critic for the *Star*.

1890

He becomes the music critic for the *World*.

1891

Shaw writes *The Quintessence of Ibsenism*, an appreciation of the playwright Henrik Ibsen.

1892

Shaw's first play, *Widower's Houses*, is performed.

1893

He writes *Mrs. Warren's Profession* and *The Philanderer*.

1894

He writes *Candida* and finishes *Arms and the Man*.

1895

Shaw becomes the theater critic for the *Saturday Review*.

1898

Shaw writes *The Perfect Wagnerite* and *Caesar and Cleopatra*.

1899

Shaw writes *Captain Brassbound's Conversion*.

1901

Queen Victoria dies.

1902

Shaw finishes *Man and Superman*.

1905

He writes *Major Barbara*.

1912

He writes *Pygmalion* and *Androcles and the Lion*.

1913

The first production of *Pygmalion* is staged in Vienna on October 16; Lucinda Shaw, the playwright's mother, dies.

1914

World War I begins; Shaw publishes *Common Sense About the War; Pygmalion* is first produced in London, with Herbert Tree and Mrs. Patrick Campbell in the starring roles.

1917

Shaw finishes *Heartbreak House*.

1926

Shaw is awarded the Nobel Prize for literature.

1938

The film of *Pygmalion* wins Shaw an Academy Award for his screenplay.

1939

World War II begins.

1943

Charlotte Shaw, the playwright's wife, dies at age eighty-six.

1950

Shaw dies on November 2.

1956

My Fair Lady, the musical, premieres.

1964

The film of *My Fair Lady* premieres.

FOR FURTHER RESEARCH

ABOUT GEORGE BERNARD SHAW

George K. Chesterton, *George Bernard Shaw.* New York: John Lane, 1909.

Archibald Henderson, *George Bernard Shaw: Man of the Century.* New York: Appleton-Century-Crofts, 1956.

Michael Holroyd, ed., *Bernard Shaw: The One-Volume Definitive Edition.* New York: Random House, 1998.

———, *The Genius of Shaw.* New York: Holt, Rinehart, and Winston, 1979.

William Irvine, *The Universe of G.B.S.* New York: Whittlesey House, 1949.

R.J. Minney, *Recollections of George Bernard Shaw.* Englewood Cliffs, NJ: Prentice-Hall, 1969.

Hesketh Pearson, *George Bernard Shaw: His Life and Personality.* New York: Atheneum, 1963.

Sally Peters, *Bernard Shaw: The Ascent of the Superman.* New Haven, CT: Yale University Press, 1996.

B.C. Rosset, *Shaw of Dublin: The Formative Years.* University Park: Pennsylvania State University Press, 1964.

Stanley Weintraub, *Journey to Heartbreak: The Crucible Years of George Bernard Shaw, 1914–1918.* New York: Weybright and Talley, 1971.

Audrey Williamson, *Bernard Shaw: Man and Writer.* New York: Crowell-Collier, 1963.

ABOUT *PYGMALION*

Charles Berst, *Bernard Shaw and the Art of Drama.* Urbana: University of Illinois Press, 1973.

John A. Bertolini, *The Playwrighting Self of Bernard Shaw.* Carbondale: Southern Illinois University Press, 1991.

Harold Bloom, ed., *George Bernard Shaw's "Pygmalion."* New York: Chelsea House, 1988.

Richard Burton, *Bernard Shaw: The Man and the Mask.* New York: Henry Holt, 1916.

Charles A. Carpenter, *Bernard Shaw and the Art of Destroying Ideals: The Early Plays.* Madison: University of Wisconsin Press, 1969.

Bernard F. Dukore, *Bernard Shaw, Playwright: Aspects of Shavian Drama.* Columbia: University of Missouri Press, 1973.

Richard Huggett, *The Truth About "Pygmalion."* London: William Heinemann, 1969.

C.D. Innes, ed., *The Cambridge Companion to George Bernard Shaw.* Cambridge, England: Cambridge University Press, 1998.

Martin Meisel, *Shaw and the Nineteenth-Century Theatre.* Princeton, NJ: Princeton University Press, 1963.

Geoffrey Miles, ed., *Classical Mythology in English Literature: A Critical Anthology.* London: Routledge, 1999.

Richard M. Ohman, *Shaw: The Style and the Man.* Middletown, CT: Wesleyan University Press, 1962.

Jean Reynolds, *Pygmalion's Wordplay: The Postmodern Shaw.* Gainesville: University of Florida Press, 1999.

Arnold Silver, *Bernard Shaw: The Darker Side.* Stanford, CA: Stanford University Press, 1982.

Rochelle Weintraub, *Fabian Feminist: Bernard Shaw and Women.* University Park: Pennsylvania State University Press, 1977.

ABOUT CLASS AND GENDER IN GREAT BRITAIN

Pamela Abbott and Roger Sapsford, *Women and Social Class.* London: Tavistock, 1987.

Ruth Adam, *A Woman's Place.* New York: Norton, 1977.

Patrick Joyce, *Visions of the People: Industrial England and the Question of Class, 1848–1914*. Cambridge, England: Cambridge University Press, 1991.

K.C. Phillipps, *Language and Class in Victorian England*. New York: Blackwell, 1984.

Jane Purvis, ed., *Women's History: Britain, 1850–1945: An Introduction*. London: Routledge, 2001.

Martha Vicinus, ed., *Suffer and Be Still: Women in the Victorian Age*. Bloomington: Indiana University Press, 1972.

INDEX